SLASH YOUR STASH

Scrap Quilts from *McCall's Quilting*

Martingale®
& COMPANY

Slash Your Stash: Scrap Quilts from *McCall's Quilting*
© 2011 by *McCall's Quilting*

That Patchwork Place® is an imprint of
Martingale & Company®.

Martingale & Company
19021 120th Ave. NE, Ste. 102
Bothell, WA 98011-9511 USA
www.martingale-pub.com

CREDITS

President & CEO: Tom Wierzbicki
Editor in Chief: Mary V. Green
Managing Editor: Tina Cook
Developmental Editor: Karen Costello Soltys
Design Director: Stan Green
Copy Editor: Sheila Chapman Ryan
Production Manager: Regina Girard
Cover and Text Designer: Stan Green
Illustrator: Laurel Strand
Photography: Supplied by *McCall's Quilting*

The information in this book is presented in good faith, but no warranty is given nor results guaranteed. *McCall's Quilting*, Martingale & Company, and Creative Crafts Group, LLC, disclaim any and all liability for untoward results.

McCall's Quilting, ISSN 1072-8395, is published bimonthly by Creative Crafts Group, LLC, 741 Corporate Circle, Suite A, Golden, CO, 80401, www.mccallsquilting.com.

Printed in China
16 15 14 13 12 11   8 7 6 5 4 3 2 1

**Library of Congress Cataloging-in-Publication Data
is available upon request.**

ISBN: 978-1-60468-070-6

MARTINGALE & COMPANY
MISSION STATEMENT
Dedicated to providing quality products and service to inspire creativity.

CONTENTS

INTRODUCTION

Scrap quilts are perennial favorites among quilt lovers of all persuasions. Quilters enjoy the mix-and-match design and sewing process, as well as the trip down Fabric Memory Lane. Quilt users are excited by the plentiful colors, patterns, and textures found in the fabrics of any scrap quilt, and by the depth and richness created by their combination. And quilt collectors relish the uniqueness of a scrappy design, the way the personality of its maker shines through, and the library of fabrics of the time included in each scrap quilt.

The conversations that begin when a scrap quilt is unfolded are often animated and sometimes sentimental. "That pink floral was from the dress my daughter wore on her first day of school." "My favorite aunt gave me a half yard of that novelty print. She used it in so many quilts of her own!" "Look at all those different shades of blue . . . how many fabrics are in this quilt altogether?" Those memories and stories and that level of excitement are special to scrap quilts alone.

The scrap-quilt patterns gathered here were chosen for their adaptability to many fabric themes and styles. It's our hope that you'll interpret these designs using your own stash fabrics, to suit your taste and complement your home. Whether your preferences are for traditional or contemporary design, small or large quilts, piecing or appliqué, and no matter what your skill level, you're sure to find quilts here to inspire a stash raid or two. And once you've finished your lovely scrap quilt, if you need a fabric-shopping trip to replenish that stash, what could be more fun?

Happy scrappy quilting!

PALACE FLOOR

Simple and sophisticated with graphic-design elements reminiscent of mosaic tile, this quilt has soft cotton prints in shades of taupe to echo the subtle patterns of fine marble. This eye-catching quilt draws the viewer in for a long, close look.

Designed by Joyce Robinson

Finished quilt size: 80¼" x 80¼"
Number of blocks and finished size: 24 Sawtooth Variation blocks, 12" x 12"

PLANNING

Joyce's design requires piecing many small triangles; be sure to use an accurate ¼" seam allowance so that your borders will be an exact fit for the quilt center. Also make sure your setting triangles are cut as half-square triangles so that the prints "read" in the same direction as Joyce's. This creates bias edges along the outside of the quilt center. Be careful not to stretch the bias edges when sewing and pressing.

FABRIC REQUIREMENTS

- Cream print (small triangles, border corner squares), 2⅜ yards
- Black solid (small triangles), 3⅝ yards
- Assorted tan, brown, green, and gray prints (blocks, setting triangles, border), 3⅝–4 yards *total*
- Brown floral print (binding), ¾ yard
- Backing, 7½ yards
- Batting, queen size

CUTTING

Cream print:
312 squares, 2⅞" x 2⅞"
8 squares, 2⅞" x 2⅞"; cut in half diagonally to make 16 half-square triangles
12 squares, 2½" x 2½"

Black solid:
528 squares, 2⅞" x 2⅞"
8 squares, 2⅞" x 2⅞"; cut in half diagonally to make 16 half-square triangles

Assorted tan, brown, green, and gray prints—cut a *total* of:
*32 squares, 8⅞" x 8⅞"; cut in half diagonally to make 64 half-square triangles
216 squares, 2⅞" x 2⅞"

Brown floral print:
9 binding strips, 2½" x 42"

*Cut first.

PIECING THE BLOCKS

❶ Draw a diagonal line on the wrong side of a cream 2⅞" square. Place the marked square on a black 2⅞" square, right sides together. Sew a ¼" seam on each side of the marked line; cut apart on the marked line. Press open to make small pieced

squares. Make 624. In the same manner, use assorted and black 2⅞" squares to make 432 total small pieced squares.

Make 624. Make 432.

❷ Sew two assorted 8⅞" half-square triangles together to make a large pieced square. Make 24 total.

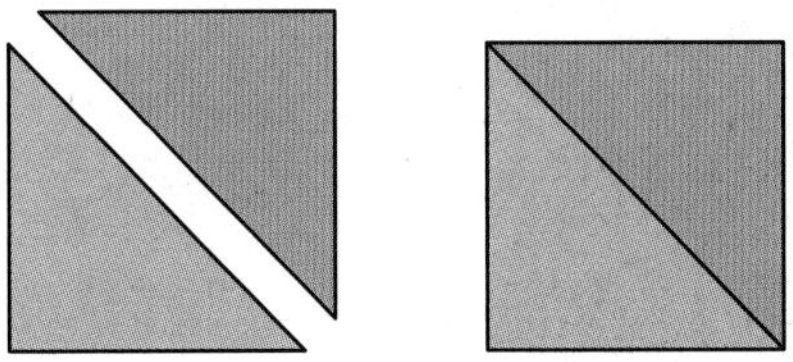

Make 24.

❸ Referring to the diagrams below, make 24 Sawtooth Variation blocks and eight of *both* setting triangles.

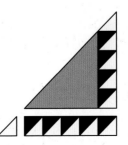

Make 24.

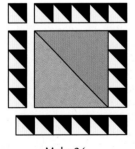

Make 8. 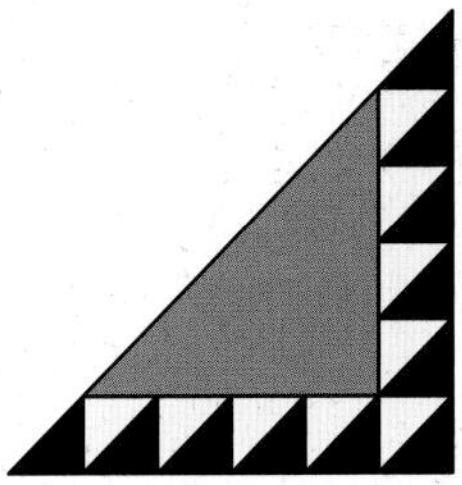   Make 8.

4 Referring to the diagram below, make four corner block sets for the outer border.

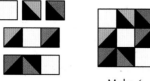

Make 4.

QUILT-TOP ASSEMBLY

Refer to the assembly diagram below for the following steps.

1 Sew six diagonal rows using the setting triangles and blocks, rotating as shown. Stitch the rows together.

2 Sew two setting triangles together to make a corner triangle. Make four. Sew these to the corners.

3 Sew 12 strips of 34 small pieced squares each, watching orientation. Sew three strips together to make a border strip. Make four. Sew strips to the sides of the quilt. Sew border corner squares to both ends of the remaining strips, and then sew them to the top and bottom of the quilt top.

QUILTING AND FINISHING

Refer to "Quiltmaking Basics" on page 90 as needed for the following steps.

1 Layer, baste, and quilt. Joyce machine quilted feathered wreaths in the block centers and quilted looping lines along the strips of small pieced squares.

2 Bind the quilt with the 2½"-wide brown floral print strips.

Assembly diagram

ENDURING ELEGANCE

When a special couple reaches a milestone anniversary, an exceptional gift is in order. This classic quilt honors lasting love with its timeless design, mix-and-match fabrics, and inviting warmth.

Designed by Lissa Alexander, machine quilted by Maggi Honeyman

Finished quilt size: 75½" x 75½"
Number of blocks and finished size: 9 Scrappy Star blocks, 17" x 17"

PLANNING

Lissa's beautiful quilt owes much of its charm to the scrappy arrangement of the fabrics. Here are some choices to consider as you plan your own version of this lovely design.

- Begin by selecting four assorted cream prints from which to cut the strips needed for the outer border. Set aside at least ½ yard of each for cutting the outer-border strips, and then move on to block fabric selection.

- For each block, choose one fabric for the large outer corner triangles, two fabrics for the four-patch units, a *brown* fabric for the star points, one or two fabrics (your choice!) for the star point backgrounds, and fabric for the center square. Cut the pieces and keep them grouped together by block as you sew. If you need help with fabric combination ideas, and feel free to experiment. Lissa even cut some of her star-point background patches as 4⅞" half-square triangles (instead of 5¼" quarter-square triangles) to keep stripes going in the same direction!

- Some of the block and middle-border patches in the featured quilt were cut from the brown polka-dot fabric used for the binding; you'll have sufficient yardage to do the same if you like. Cut the binding strips first, and then any pieces desired.

- Our instructions for the inner border direct you to cut and stitch together 15 strips, 2" x 18", and then cut the border lengths needed. For a more random look, consider using 2"-wide strips of varied lengths, creating a pieced strip at least 225" (6¼ yards) long. From this strip, cut the lengths specified in step 2 of "Quilt-Top Assembly" on page 13.

FABRIC REQUIREMENTS

- Assorted brown prints (blocks, middle border), 1½–1¾ yards *total*
- Assorted dark pink prints (blocks), ⅛–¼ yard *total*
- Assorted blue prints (blocks, inner and middle borders), 1–1¼ yards *total*
- Assorted cream and tan prints (blocks, borders) 4¼–4½ yards *total*
- Assorted pink prints (blocks, inner and middle borders), ¾–1 yard *total*
- Brown polka-dot print (binding), 1 yard
- Backing, 4¾ yards
- Batting, queen size

CUTTING

See "Planning" above before cutting.

*For the outer border, cut:
   4 strips, 8" x 80", pieced from *4 sets of 2* matching cream print strips, 8" x 42"

For each block, cut:
   *Corner triangles: 2 matching squares, 9⅜" x 9⅜"; cut in half diagonally to make 4 half-square triangles
   Four-patch units: *2 sets of 8* matching squares, 2½" x 2½" (16 total)
   Star points: 2 matching brown squares, 5¼" x 5¼"
   Star-point backgrounds: 2 squares, 5¼" x 5¼"
   Center: 1 square, 4½" x 4½"

For the inner border, cut:
   15 assorted cream, tan, blue, and pink strips, 2" x 18"

For the middle border, cut:
   38 assorted brown squares, 3⅞" x 3⅞"
   38 assorted cream, tan, blue, and pink squares, 3⅞" x 3⅞"

For the binding, cut:
   9 brown polka-dot strips, 2½" x 42"

*Cut first.

PIECING THE BLOCKS AND BORDER UNITS

1. Using two sets of eight matching 2½" squares, stitch four matching four-patch units. Make nine sets total, one set for each block.

2. Draw a diagonal line from corner to corner in each direction on the wrong side of an assorted 5¼" star-point background square. Place the marked square on a brown 5¼" star-point square, right sides together. Sew a ¼"-wide seam on each side of one line. Cutting on the *unsewn* line first, then on the remaining drawn line, cut the sewn square into quarters. Press open to make pieced triangles. Make eight total with matching brown patches for each block.

Make 9 sets of 8 total.

3. Stitch together two pieced triangles with matching brown patches to make a star-point square. Make four matching for each block.

Make 9 sets of 4 matching units.

4. Use four matching four-patch units, four matching star-point squares, and an assorted 4½" square to sew three rows. Stitch the rows together to make the block center. Make nine.

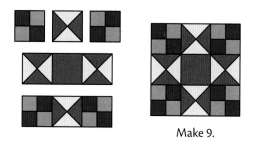

Make 9.

5. Sew four matching 9⅜" half-square triangles to the block center to complete a Scrappy Star block. Make nine.

Make 9.

6. Draw a diagonal line on the wrong side of an assorted cream, tan, blue, or pink 3⅞" square. Place the marked square on an assorted brown 3⅞" square, right sides together. Sew a ¼" seam on each side of the marked line; cut apart on the marked line. Press open to make pieced squares. Make 76; set 4 aside for the border corners.

Make 76; set 4 aside.

7. Sew two pieced squares together to make a border rectangle. Make 36.

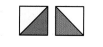

Make 36.

QUILT-TOP ASSEMBLY

Refer to the assembly diagram below for the following steps.

1. Sew three rows of three blocks each. Sew the rows together.

2. Using diagonal seams as shown, stitch the 15 assorted 2" x 18" strips together end to end. From the pieced strip, cut the following lengths:
   - 1 strip, 51½"
   - 2 strips, 53" each
   - 1 strip, 54½"

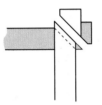

3. Sew the 51½" strip to the bottom of the quilt center, sew the 53" strips to the left side and top of the quilt center, and sew the 54½" strip to the right side of the quilt center, in that order.

4. To make the middle border, sew nine border rectangles together end to end. Make four total.

Sew strips to opposite sides of the quilt. Watching orientation, stitch the border corner squares to the ends of the remaining strips; sew to the top and bottom of the quilt.

5. Starting and stopping ¼" from the quilt corners, stitch the 8" x 80" outer-border strips to the sides, top, and bottom of the quilt, centering them. Sew and trim the mitered corners, referring to "Mitered Borders" on page 94 as needed.

QUILTING AND FINISHING

Refer to "Quiltmaking Basics" on page 90 as needed for the following steps.

1. Layer, baste, and quilt. Maggi machine quilted swirls across the four-patch units and centers of the blocks. The star points were outline quilted and the star-point background triangles were stitched with a swirling meander. The block corner triangles and the outer border were filled with feathers. The brown border triangles feature double curved lines.

2. Bind the quilt with the 2½"-wide brown polka-dot strips.

Assembly diagram

SUMMER SHADOWS

Joyce began this quilt by picking a few scrap fabrics that she really liked, and then the rest of the scraps she chose had to look good with the first ones. She stayed away from really bright colors, and kept auditioning scraps to see if they looked good together.

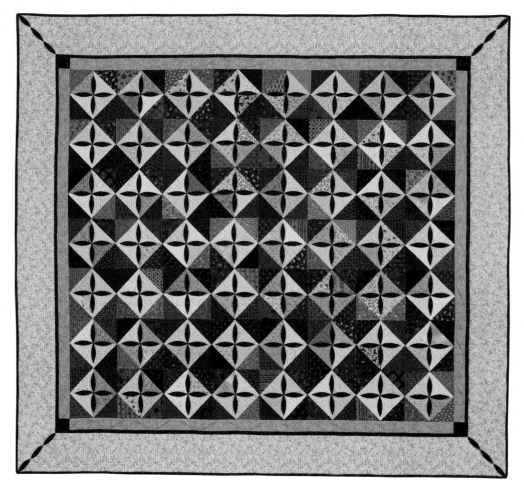

Designed by Joyce Stewart; machine quilted by Virginia Gore

Finished quilt size: 91½" x 101½"
Number of blocks and finished size: 56 Petal blocks, 10" x 10"

PLANNING

Divide your stash into light and medium/dark fabrics, aiming for high value contrast between the two piles. The more contrast there is, the more dramatic the design. Any and all color families work with this scrappy design. Look closely at Joyce's quilt and you'll find every color of the color wheel. The trick when using so many colors is to choose textural prints that are subdued, not splashy. Choose a small, dark, tone-on-tone print for the appliqué petals so their curved edges stand out against the light prints.

FABRIC REQUIREMENTS

- Assorted light prints (blocks), 3¼–3¾ yards *total*
- Assorted dark prints (blocks), 3¼–3¾ yards *total*
- Brown print (petals, middle border, border corners, binding), 2⅝ yards
- Gold print (inner border), ⅞ yard
- Cream-and-green print (outer border), 3⅛ yards
- Backing (piece widthwise), 8½ yards
- Batting, king size

CUTTING

The appliqué patterns are on page 17. You can prepare the appliqués for fusible web or for hand appliqué. The appliqué patterns are printed without seam allowance, so be sure to add a seam allowance as you cut them for hand appliqué.

Assorted light prints—cut a *total* of:
   112 squares, 5⅞" x 5⅞"

Assorted dark prints—cut a *total* of:
   112 squares, 5⅞" x 5⅞"

Brown print:
   *9 strips, 1¼" x 42"
   *10 binding strips, 2½" x 42"
   224 using template A
   12 using template B
   4 squares, 3½" x 3½"

Gold print:
   9 strips, 2¾" x 42"

Cream-and-green print:
   4 strips, 8" x 105", cut on the *lengthwise* grain
*Cut first.

PIECING AND APPLIQUÉING THE BLOCKS

1 Draw a diagonal line from corner to corner on the wrong side of a light print 5⅞" square. Place the marked square on a dark print square, right sides together. Sew a ¼" on each side of the marked line; cut apart on the marked line. Press open to make pieced squares. Make 224.

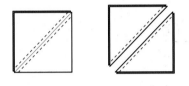
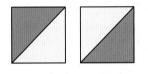

Make 224.

2 Stitch together four pieced squares to make a block background, positioning the pieced squares so the light patches meet in the center. Make 56.

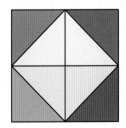

Make 56.

3 Using the seam lines as a placement guide, position four A pieces on a block with the petals touching in the center. Fuse or hand appliqué in place. Joyce finished her petal edges with machine feather stitching in variegated brown thread. Make 56 Petal blocks.

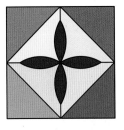 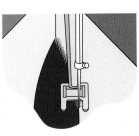

Make 56.

QUILT-TOP ASSEMBLY

Refer to the assembly diagram at right for the following steps.

1 Sew eight rows of seven blocks each. Sew the rows together.

2 Sew the nine 2¾"-wide gold strips together end to end; from this long strip, cut four border strips, 84" long. Repeat for the 1¼"-wide brown strips. Sew the gold and brown strips together to make four pieced strips. Measure the exact width of the quilt from raw edge to raw edge; trim two of the pieced strips to this measurement and sew a 3½" brown square to each end. Measure the exact length of the quilt and trim the remaining two strips to this length. Sew these strips to the sides of the quilt top, with the gold strips adjoining the quilt top. Sew the remaining strips to the top and bottom of the quilt.

3 Starting and stopping ¼" from the quilt corners, stitch the cream-and-green strips to each side of the quilt top, centering them. Sew and trim the mitered corners, referring to "Mitered Borders" on page 94 as needed.

4 Referring to the quilt photo and using the mitered seams as a placement guide, position three B pieces on each corner of the cream-and-green borders. Appliqué in place.

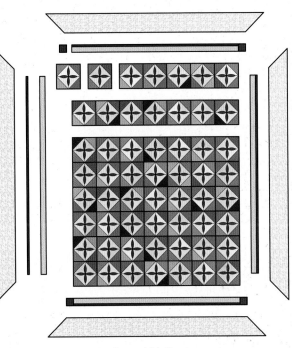

Assembly diagram

QUILTING AND FINISHING

Refer to "Quiltmaking Basics" on page 90 as needed for the following steps.

1 Layer, baste, and quilt. Virginia used a puffy batting and gold thread. She machine outline quilted around the petals and repeated the petal shape between petals and in the corner triangles of the blocks. She added a continuous swirl in the inner border and filled the outer border with a repeating flower-and-leaf design.

2 Bind the quilt with the 2½"-wide brown print strips. The inner edge of the binding on the featured quilt is finished from the front with machine feather stitching.

A
Cut 224 from brown print.

B
Cut 12 from brown print.

RAMBLING ROSE

Get a jump start on spring by appliquéing the sweetest roses imaginable on this matching wall hanging and table runner. The bees are already buzzing about this beautiful duo—and soon your friends will be too.

Designed by Pat Sloan

Finished wall hanging size: 40½" x 40½" ● **Finished table runner size: 14" x 32½"**

WALL HANGING

FABRIC REQUIREMENTS

- Assorted beige prints (background piecing), 1–1¼ yards *total*
- Dark green plaid (center stems), 14" x 14" piece
- Assorted pink prints, stripes, and plaids (flowers, buds), ½–¾ yard *total*
- Yellow mottled print (flower centers), 5" x 20" piece
- Gold-and-yellow mottled print (flower centers), 4" x 14" piece
- Assorted dark green prints, stripes, and plaids (buds, leaves), ¼–⅜ yard *total*
- Gold mottled print (circles, bees), ¼ yard
- Green-and-tan striped fabric (inner border, leaves, binding), 1 yard
- Dark green small floral striped fabric (outer border), ¾ yard
- Dark green checked fabric (outer-border corners), 13" x 13" piece
- Light green checked fabric (border vine), 17" x 17" piece
- Light green print (border leaves), 12" x 12" piece
- Brown-and-beige striped fabric (bee wings), 6" x 10" piece
- Black solid (bee stripes), 5" x 5" piece
- Backing, 2⅝ yards
- Batting, crib size
- Bias bar, ⅜" (optional)

CUTTING

Assorted beige prints—cut a *total* of:
   16 squares, 7⅞" x 7⅞"

Dark green plaid:
   1¼"-wide bias-cut strips, enough to yield 75" (see "Planning" above)

Assorted pink prints, stripes, and plaids:
   6 sets of 2 matching using template A (12 total)
   6 sets of 3 matching using template A (18 total)
   5 using template D

Yellow mottled print:
   6 using template B

Gold-and-yellow mottled print:
   6 using template C

Assorted dark green prints, stripes, and plaids—cut a *total* of:
   5 using template E
   7 using template F

Gold mottled print:
   27 using template G
   4 using template I

Green-and-tan striped fabric:
   *4 strips, 1½" x 35"
   2½"-wide bias-cut strips, enough to yield 50" of binding (see "Planning")
   5 using template F

Dark green small floral striped fabric:
   4 strips, 5½" x 42"

Dark green checked fabric:
   4 squares, 5½" x 5½"

Light green checked fabric:
   1¼"-wide bias-cut strips, enough to yield 155" (see "Planning")

Light green print:
   8 using template F

Brown-and-beige striped fabric:
   4 using template H

Black solid:
   4 *each* using templates J and K

*Cut first.

PIECING AND APPLIQUÉING THE BACKGROUND

❶ On the wrong side of a beige print 7⅞" square, draw a diagonal line with the marking tool of your choice. Place the marked square on another assorted beige print 7⅞" square, right sides together. Sew a ¼" seam on each side of the marked line; cut the squares apart on the marked line. Press the triangles open to make pieced squares. Repeat to make 16 total.

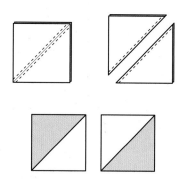

Make 16.

❷ Arrange and sew four rows of four pieced squares each. Sew the rows together to make the pieced background square.

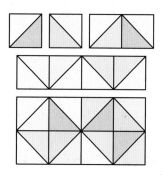

❸ For the flower stems, fold the dark green plaid 1¼" x 75" bias strip in half, wrong sides together. Stitch ¼" from the raw edge. Trim the seam allowance to ⅛". Press the bias tube flat, centering the seam allowance on the back so the raw edges aren't visible from the front. Using a ⅜"-wide bias bar makes pressing faster and easier.

❹ Cut flower stems from the dark green plaid bias tube in the following lengths: two 12" sections, one 13½", one 11½", and one 9½". For the bud stems, cut the following: one 3¾", one 3", one 2½", and two 2¼". Repeat the sewing process for the border vine using the light green checked 1¼" x 155" bias-cut strip. Set the bias tube aside for the border appliqué.

❺ Using the seam lines of the pieced background square as placement guides and the assembly diagram on page 21 for reference, position the flower stems, bud stems, and appliqués A–K. Using the appliqué method of your choice (see "Quiltmaking Basics" on page 90), appliqué the pieces in place.

WALL-HANGING ASSEMBLY

Refer to the assembly diagram for the following steps.

❶ Sew green-and-tan striped 1½" x 35" strips to the sides of the quilt top; trim them even with the top and bottom of the quilt. Stitch the remaining green-and-tan striped strips to the top and bottom of the quilt top; trim even with the sides. Press the seam allowances toward the borders.

❷ Measure the exact width of the wall hanging (from raw edge to raw edge). Trim two dark green floral striped 5½" strips to this measurement and sew a dark green checked 5½" square to each end of the strips. Sew the untrimmed dark green floral striped strips to the sides of the quilt top; trim even with the top and bottom of the quilt. Sew the pieced border strips to the top and bottom of the quilt. Press the seam allowances toward the green borders. Referring to the photo on page 18, appliqué the light green checked vine and remaining appliqués to the border.

Wall-hanging assembly diagram

QUILTING AND FINISHING THE WALL HANGING

Refer to "Quiltmaking Basics" on page 90 as needed for the following steps.

1. Layer and baste the quilt top for the quilting method of your choice. Pat machine quilted in the ditch around the appliqué shapes and flower centers. She added a wavy line in the inner border and filled the background and outer border with meander stitching.

2. Bind the quilt with the 2½"-wide green-and-tan striped bias strips.

3. Add a hanging sleeve.

TABLE RUNNER

Stitch this coordinating table runner to display with the wall hanging for a nice dining-room or foyer ensemble.

FABRIC REQUIREMENTS

- Dark green checked fabric (background), ½ yard
- Light green plaid (stems), 10" x 10" square
- Assorted pink prints, stripes, and plaids (flowers), ¼–⅜ yard *total*
- Yellow mottled print (flower centers), 8" x 9" piece
- Gold-and-yellow mottled print (flower centers), 6" x 6" piece
- Light green print (leaves), 7" x 12" piece
- Green-and-tan striped fabric (leaf, bias-cut binding), 18" x 20" piece
- Gold mottled print (circles, bee body), 8" x 10" piece
- Brown-and-beige striped fabric (bee wings), 3" x 5" piece
- Black solid (bee stripes), 3" x 3" piece
- Backing, ⅝ yard
- Batting, 20" x 39" piece
- Bias bar, ⅜" (optional)

CUTTING

Appliqué patterns are on pages 24–26 and do not include seam allowances.

Dark green checked fabric:
   1 using template L
Light green plaid:
   2 bias-cut strips, 1¼" x 8½" (see "Planning" on page 19)
Assorted pink prints, stripes, and plaids:
   3 sets of 2 matching using template A
   3 sets of 3 matching using template A
Yellow mottled print:
   3 using template B
Gold-and-yellow mottled print:
   3 using template C
Light green print:
   3 using template F
Green-and-tan striped fabric:
   1 using template F
Gold mottled print:
   9 using template G
   1 using template I
Brown-and-beige striped fabric:
   1 using template H
Black solid:
   1 *each* using templates J and K

APPLIQUÉING THE TABLE RUNNER

① Referring to step 3 of "Piecing and Appliquéing the Background" on page 20, make two light green plaid 8½" bias flower stems.

② Finger-press the dark green checked piece L in half lengthwise and widthwise; use the folds as a placement guide. Referring to the assembly diagram below, position the appliqués.

③ Using your appliqué method of choice, appliqué the pieces in place. Using thread that matches the fabric, blanket-stitch the appliqués by hand or machine, if desired.

QUILTING AND FINISHING THE TABLE RUNNER

Refer to "Quiltmaking Basics" on page 90 as needed for the following steps.

① Layer and baste the table runner top for the quilting method of your choice. Pat machine quilted in the ditch around the appliqués and added a meander to the background.

② Bind the table runner with the bias-cut green-and-tan striped fabric.

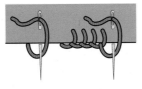

Blanket stitch

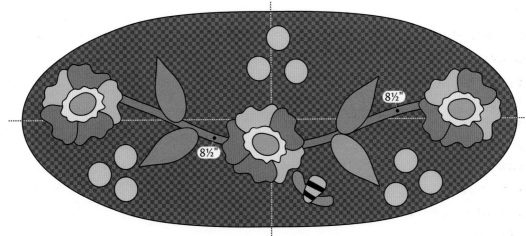

Table-runner assembly diagram

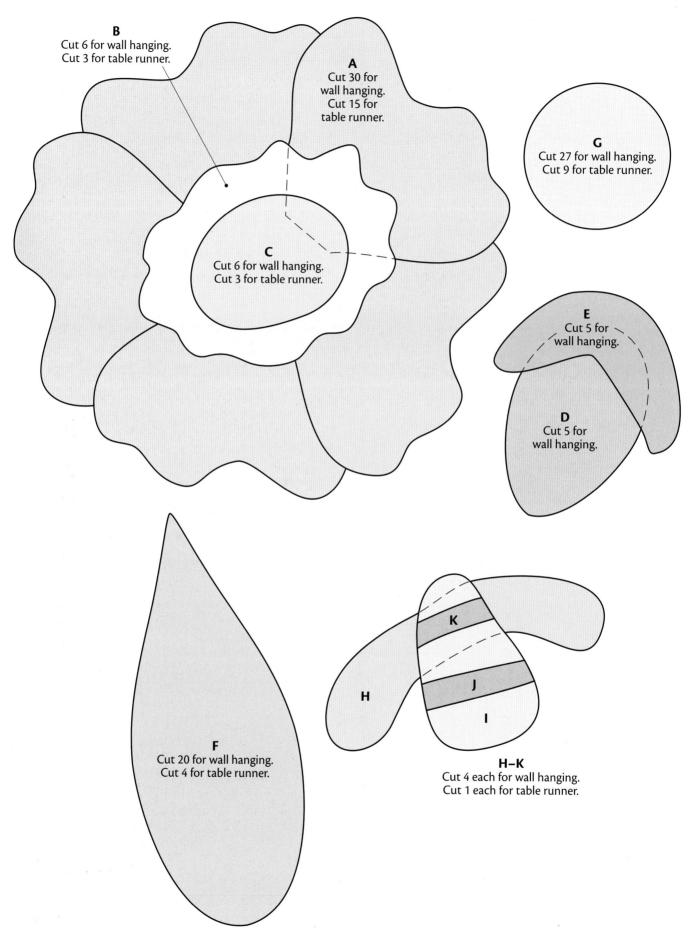

B
Cut 6 for wall hanging.
Cut 3 for table runner.

A
Cut 30 for
wall hanging.
Cut 15 for
table runner.

G
Cut 27 for wall hanging.
Cut 9 for table runner.

C
Cut 6 for wall hanging.
Cut 3 for table runner.

E
Cut 5 for
wall hanging.

D
Cut 5 for
wall hanging.

K

J

H

I

H–K
Cut 4 each for wall hanging.
Cut 1 each for table runner.

F
Cut 20 for wall hanging.
Cut 4 for table runner.

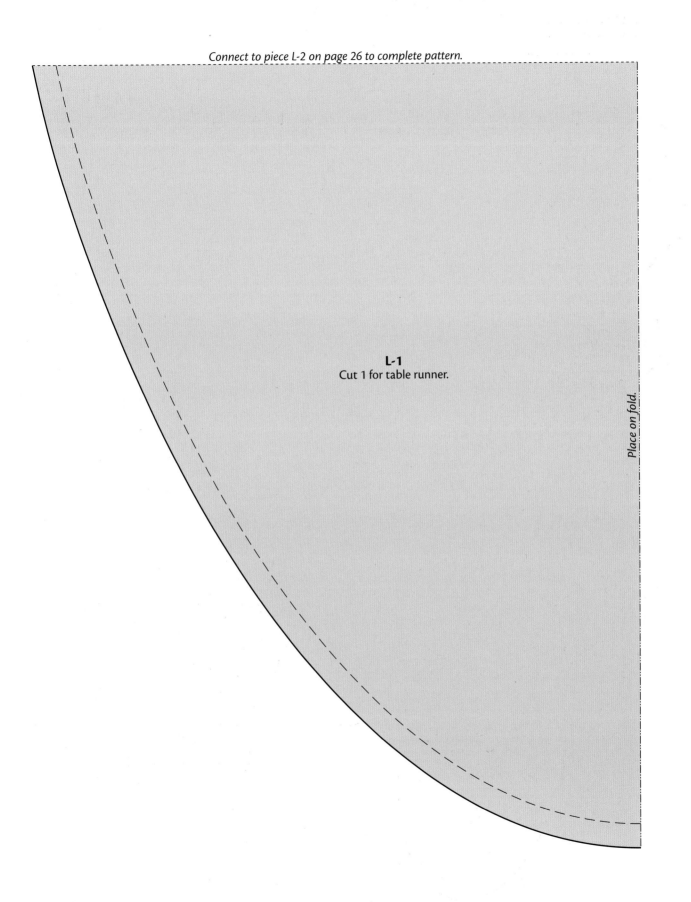

Connect to piece L-2 on page 26 to complete pattern.

L-1
Cut 1 for table runner.

Place on fold.

Place on fold.

L-2

Connect to piece L-1 on page 25 to complete pattern.

PRAIRIE BASKETS

Create a quilt just like the one you remember that covered Grandma's bed. It's easy to do with a classic basket pattern and vintage-inspired fabrics such as small checks and calicoes. This combination is sure to evoke warm, happy memories.

Designed by Laura DeMarco and Rita DeMarco; machine quilted by Ardis Young

Finished quilt size: 84¼" x 101¼"
Number of blocks and finished size: 20 Basket blocks, 12" x 12"

In each Basket block, a checked or striped fabric is paired with a floral fabric, creating a stunning combination. We instruct you to do as Laura and Rita did—make two blocks from each fabric combination. The block pairs will have reverse colorations.

FABRIC REQUIREMENTS

A fat quarter is an 18" x 20"–22" cut of fabric.

- 10 assorted checked and striped fabrics (baskets), 1 fat quarter each
- 10 assorted floral prints (baskets), 1 fat quarter each
- Ivory print (block background), 2 yards
- Rose-and-gold plaid (setting triangles), 1½ yards
- Yellow small floral (setting squares), 1⅝ yards
- Red print (inner border, corners), 1 yard
- Yellow-and-rose striped floral print (outer border), 2⅝ yards
- Gold checked fabric (bias binding), 1⅛ yards
- Backing (piece widthwise), 7¾ yards
- Batting, queen size
- Bias bar, ⅜" (optional)

CUTTING

The pattern for A and A reversed is on page 31.

10 assorted checked/striped fabrics and 10 assorted florals—cut from *each*:

*1 bias strip, 1¼" x 16" (20 total)

6 squares, 2⅞" x 2⅞" (120 total)

3 squares, 2⅞" x 2⅞"; cut in half diagonally to make 6 half-square triangles (120 total)

Ivory print:

*10 squares, 12⅞" x 12⅞"; cut in half diagonally to make 20 half-square triangles

20 *each* using template A and A reversed

10 squares, 4⅞" x 4⅞"; cut in half diagonally to make 20 half-square triangles

Rose-and-gold plaid:

*4 squares, 19" x 19"; cut into quarters diagonally to make 16 quarter-square triangles (2 left over)

2 squares, 10" x 10"; cut in half diagonally to make 4 half-square triangles

Yellow small floral:

12 squares, 12½" x 12½"

Red print:

*9 strips, 2½" x 42"

4 squares, 6½" x 6½"

Yellow-and-rose striped floral print, cut on the *lengthwise* grain:

2 strips, 6½" x 76"

2 strips, 6½" x 92"

Gold checked fabric:

2½"-wide bias strips, enough to yield 385" of binding

Cut first.

PIECING AND APPLIQUÉING THE BLOCKS

1 On the wrong side of a checked or striped 2⅞" square, draw a diagonal line using the marking tool of your choice. Place the marked square on a floral 2⅞" square, right sides together. Sew a ¼" seam on each side of the marked line; cut apart the squares on the marked line. Press the triangles open to make pieced squares. Make 10 sets of 12 matching pieced squares.

Make 10 sets of 12 matching units.

2 Sew a matching pair of assorted 2⅞" triangles to ivory A and A reversed pieces as shown. Make 20 of each, using each checked and striped fabric for only one pair.

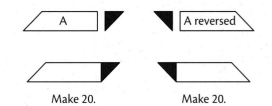

Make 20.   Make 20.

❸ Carefully arrange and stitch together six matching pieced squares and two matching 2⅞" half-square triangles to make a large pieced triangle. Add the A and A reversed units to the short sides of the pieced triangle and an ivory 4⅞" half-square triangle to the corner to make the basket bottom. Make 20.

Make 20.

❹ Fold the assorted 1¼" x 16" bias strips in half, wrong sides together. Stitch ¼" from the raw edges. Trim the seam allowances to ⅛". Press the tubes flat, centering the seam allowances on the back so that the raw edges aren't visible from the front. Using a ⅜" bias bar makes pressing faster and easier. Make 20.

❺ Place a prepared bias basket handle on an ivory 12⅞" half-square triangle, positioning the ends 3½" in from the corner so that the outer edges will meet at or just inside the basket corners when the handle triangle is stitched to the basket bottom using a ¼" seam allowance, as shown. Using your appliqué method of choice, appliqué the

handle in place. Trim the ends of the handle strip if necessary.

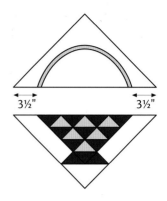

❻ Sew the appliquéd handle triangle to the basket bottom to complete a Basket block, taking care not to stretch the bias edges. Make 20.

Make 20.

QUILT-TOP ASSEMBLY

Refer to the assembly diagram on page 31 for the following steps. The setting triangles on all edges and corners are cut slightly oversized to allow for trimming the quilt-top edges even after assembly, before adding the borders.

❶ Arrange and sew eight diagonal rows using the rose-and-gold plaid 19" quarter-square triangles, the blocks, and the yellow small floral 12½" squares. Sew the rows together. Press the seam allowances toward the yellow squares and plaid triangles. Stitch rose-and-gold plaid 10" half-square triangles to the quilt corners. Press, and then trim the quilt edges even.

❷ Sew the red print 2½" strips together end to end to make a long strip. Cut two strips, 88" long, and sew them to the quilt sides; press, and then trim them even with the top and bottom of the quilt. From the remaining long strip, cut two strips, 76" long, and sew them to the top and bottom of the quilt; press, and then trim even with the sides of the quilt.

3 Measure the exact width of the quilt (raw edge to raw edge). Trim the two yellow-and-rose floral 6½" x 76" strips to the exact width measurement; sew a red print 6½" square to each end of the trimmed strips. Stitch the untrimmed yellow-and-rose floral 6½" x 92" strips to the sides of the quilt top; press, and then trim them even with the top and bottom of the quilt. Sew the pieced strips to the top and bottom of the quilt. Press.

Assembly diagram

QUILTING AND FINISHING

Refer to "Quiltmaking Basics" on page 90 as needed for the following steps.

1 Layer and baste the quilt top for the quilting method of your choice. Ardis machine quilted this quilt, outlining each basket patch with a curved line. She centered a three-leaf motif inside each basket handle. A close meander covers the remaining block backgrounds. A continuous, flowing feather fills each setting square and triangle and is repeated in the outer border. The inner border features a loop design.

2 Bind the quilt with the gold checked bias-cut strips.

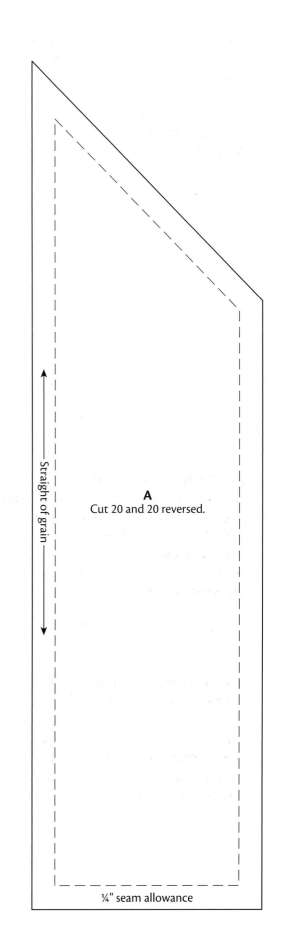

Straight of grain

A
Cut 20 and 20 reversed.

¼" seam allowance

JACK IN THE PULPIT

Elaine's quilting bee (the Fussy Cutters from Huntsville, Alabama) has a block swap of some kind each year. This particular swap allowed members to choose a block they wanted for their own quilt. Elaine wanted the finished product to look like it came out of an old cedar chest, so she requested everyone to make the blocks out of scrappy reds (as close to 1800s fabrics as possible) and to use the Jack in the Pulpit pattern. She now has a one-of-a-kind quilt made with her quilting friends.

Designed by Elaine McGarry

Finished quilt size: 76" x 88½"

Number of blocks and finished size: 20 Jack in the Pulpit blocks, 10" x 10"

Raid your friends' stashes—and your own—to find a variety of prints in your favorite shades of red. Choose a mix of both busy and quiet prints for added texture and interest. Notice that Elaine substituted white prints for the cream prints in a few places for a bit of sparkle.

The flying-geese units in the middle border are constructed in two different ways. The side geese are made with a quick-piecing technique, and the top and bottom geese as well as the block centers are foundation pieced to ensure an accurate fit. A knowledge of foundation piecing (paper piecing) is required for this pattern. (For a review of foundation-piecing techniques, visit the *McCall's Quilting* website at mccallsquilting.com, click on "Lessons," and then click on "Piece by Piece.")

Elaine fussy cut her outer-border strips so all four are identical. This allowed her to place the same stripe toward the outside on all sides of the quilt. Do likewise if you wish.

Be sure to use an accurate ¼" seam throughout to ensure that the pieced border fits well.

HINT: If you have trouble removing the paper after foundation piecing, mist the back of a unit with a spray bottle filled with water and allow it to sit for 10 minutes before paper removal. Test first on the lightest fabric and printed foundation to be sure the misted ink doesn't transfer to the fabric.

FABRIC REQUIREMENTS

- Assorted red prints (blocks, middle border), 3¾–4¼ yards *total*
- Assorted cream prints (blocks, middle border), 3¾–3¼ yards *total*
- Brown print (sashing, inner border), 1⅝ yards
- Tan-and-brown dot print (sashing posts), ⅛ yard
- Red striped fabric (outer border, bias-cut binding), 3¼ yards
- Backing (piece widthwise), 7¼ yards
- Batting, queen size

CUTTING

Assorted red prints:

Cut 20 *matching sets* of:
    1 square, 4" x 4" (20 total)
    2 strips, 2¼" x 5½" (40 total)
    2 strips, 2¼" x 8¼" (40 total)
    2 squares, 3⅜" x 3⅜"; cut in half diagonally to
        make 4 half-square triangles (80 total)

Cut 4 sets of:
    4 matching squares, 3" x 3" (16 total)

Cut a *total* of:
    52 rectangles, 3" x 5½"
    44 rectangles, 3½" x 7"

Assorted cream prints:

Cut 20 *matching sets* of:
    2 squares, 3½" x 3½"; cut in half diagonally to
        make 4 half-square triangles (80 total)
    6 squares, 3⅜" x 3⅜"; cut squares in half
        diagonally to make 12 half-square
        triangles (240 total)

Cut 52 sets of:
    2 matching squares, 3" x 3" (104 total)

Cut a *total* of:
    44 squares, 4¼" x 4¼"; cut in half diagonally to
        make 44 sets of 2 matching half-square
        triangles (88 total)
    4 squares, 5½" x 5½"

Brown print:
    *7 strips, 3" x 42"
    31 strips, 3" x 10½"

Tan-and-brown dot print:
    12 squares, 3" x 3"

Red striped fabric:
    4 strips, 7" x 80", cut on the *lengthwise* grain
        (see "Planning" above)
    1 square, 31" x 31"; sew and cut 2½"-wide
        continuous bias-cut binding from the
        square (see page 95)

*Cut first.

PIECING THE BLOCKS AND BORDER UNITS

Foundation patterns are on pages 36 and 37.

1 Use one matching set each of cream and red patches per block. Make 20 copies of foundation pattern A on page 37. Referring to the pattern for fabric placement, foundation piece units for the block centers. Make 20 block centers total. Trim the excess fabric along the outer dashed lines. To stabilize any bias edges, do not remove the paper until instructed (after adding the outer border).

Make 20.

2 Sew together three matching cream 3⅜" half-square triangles and one red 3⅜" half-square triangle to make a block corner as shown. Make four matching block corners and stitch them to a matching block center to make a Jack in the Pulpit block. Make 20 total.

Make 20.

3 Draw a diagonal line on the wrong side of a cream 3" square. Place the marked square on a red 3" x 5½" rectangle, right sides together and raw edges aligned as shown. Sew on the drawn line; trim away and discard the excess fabric. Using a matching cream 3" square, repeat on the other end of the rectangle to make a side-border flying-geese unit. Make 52 total.

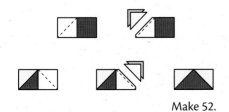

Make 52.

4 Make 44 copies of foundation pattern B. Referring to the pattern for fabric placement, foundation piece units for the top and bottom middle border. Make 44 top/bottom units total. Trim the excess fabric along the outer dashed lines around all sides of the units. To help stabilize any bias edges, do not remove the paper until instructed (after adding the outer border).

5 Draw a diagonal line on the wrong side of an assorted red 3" square. Place the marked square on an assorted cream 5½" square, right sides together and aligning raw edges. Sew on the marked line; trim away and discard the excess fabric. Press open. Repeat with matching red squares on the remaining corners to make a border-corner square. Make four total.

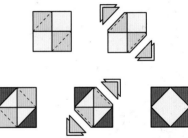

Make 4.

QUILT-TOP ASSEMBLY

Refer to the assembly diagram on page 36 for the following steps.

1 Sew five block rows using four blocks and three brown 10½" strips each. Stitch four sashing rows using four brown 10½" strips and three tan-and-brown dot squares each. Sew the block and sashing rows together, alternating them as shown.

2 Sew three of the brown 3" strips together end to end. From this long strip, cut two 48"-long strips and sew them to the top and bottom of the quilt. Sew the remaining four brown 3" strips together end to end and from the strip, cut two 65½"-long strips; sew them to the quilt sides.

3 To make side pieced border strips, stitch together 26 flying-geese units (made in step 3 of "Piecing the Blocks and Border Units" on page 35), reversing their orientation at the middle of the strip. Make two strips and stitch them to the sides of the quilt. To make the top and bottom pieced border strips, stitch together 22 foundation-pieced units, reversing the orientation at the middle of the strip. Make two and add border-corner squares to the ends. Stitch the borders to the top and bottom of the quilt.

4 Sew the red striped 80"-long strips to the sides of the quilt; trim them even with the top and bottom of the quilt. Sew the remaining red striped strips to the top and bottom of the quilt; trim even with the quilt sides. Remove the paper from the back of the foundation-pieced units. See "Hint" on page 33."

QUILTING AND FINISHING

Refer to "Quiltmaking Basics" on page 90 as needed for the following steps.

1 Layer, baste, and quilt. Elaine hand outline quilted all the patches in the middle border. She quilted a diagonal grid in the center red squares of the blocks and a four-cornered leaf-and-wave motif in the remainder. A double X is stitched in the tan sashing post squares and a double cable in the sashing and brown inner border. The outer border is quilted with parallel lines spaced 1¼" apart, perpendicular to the quilt edges.

2 Bind the quilt with the 2½"-wide bias-cut red striped fabric.

Assembly diagram

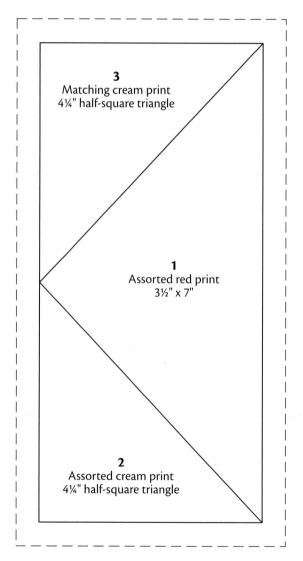

Foundation Pattern B
Make 44 copies.

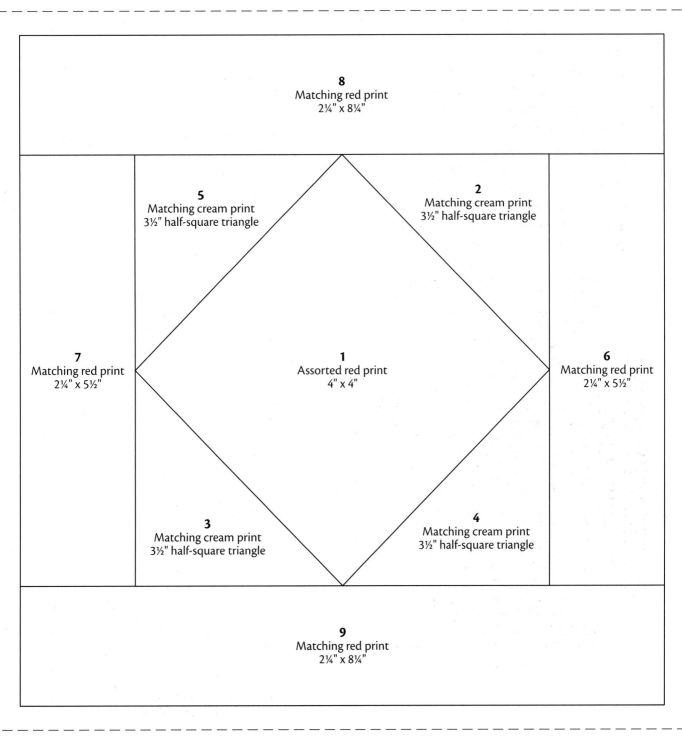

Foundation Pattern A
Make 20 copies.

TAILGATE

Snuggle in the football stands or curl up in front of the fireplace with this colorful throw. Even big, strong men appreciate a comfy quilt at a chilly game or picnic. This bright flannel throw will keep him warm, and can be easily adapted to any team's colors if desired.

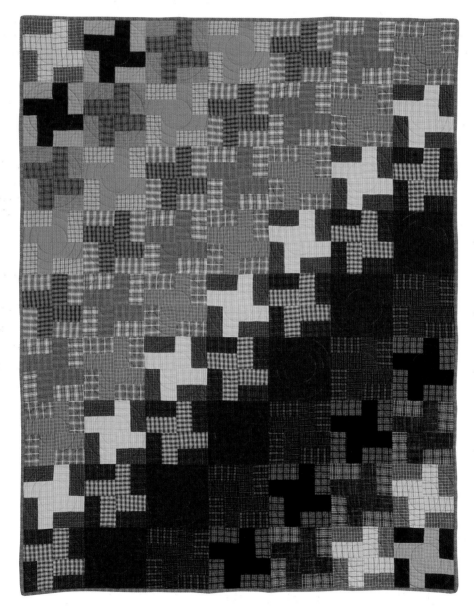

Designed by Catherine Purifoy

Finished quilt size: 56½" x 72½"
Number of blocks and finished size: 63 Endless Stairs Variation blocks, 8" x 8"

For each block, Catherine chose two fabrics that share a color, and she placed the blocks in a diagonal rainbow arrangement when assembling the quilt. Our pattern instructs you to cut and sew seven blocks of each fabric combination. This is more than are needed for the quilt, so you can experiment with alternate arrangements until you find the one most pleasing to your eye. Extra blocks can be used for another project, or you can plan your arrangement in advance and make only the blocks needed for your version of the quilt.

You'll need full 18" x 20"–22" fat quarters to cut the strips required; we recommend you not prewash before cutting, due to possible shrinkage of flannel fabrics.

FABRIC REQUIREMENTS

A fat quarter is an 18" x 20"–22" cut of fabric.

- *26 assorted plaid and solid flannels (blocks), 1 fat quarter *each*

- Turquoise plaid flannel (binding), ⅝ yard

- Backing (piece widthwise), 3⅝ yards

- Batting, twin size

See "Planning" above.

CUTTING

26 assorted plaid and solid flannels—cut from each:
7 strips, 2½" x 20" (182 total)

Turquoise plaid flannel:
8 binding strips, 2½" x 42"

PIECING THE BLOCKS

❶ Sew together two different plaid or solid 20" strips to make a strip set. Press the seam allowances toward the darker fabric. Make seven identical strip sets and cut 28 segments, 4½" wide. Repeat with the remaining 20" plaid and solid strips to make 13 fabric combinations total.

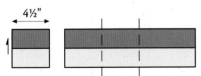

4½"

Make 7 strip sets from each
of 13 fabric combinations (91 total).
Cut 28 segments of each combination.

❷ Sew together four matching segments to make an Endless Stairs Variation block. Make seven matching blocks. Repeat to make seven blocks in each fabric combination for a total of 91 blocks.

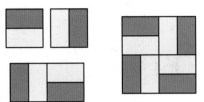

Make 7 each
of 13 fabric combinations
(91 total).

WAIT TO PRESS

You may want to wait to do the final pressing of each completed block until you've planned the block layout for your quilt. That way you can press the center seam allowances in each block in the opposite direction from the seam allowances in the adjacent block, which will make sewing them together much easier.

QUILT-TOP ASSEMBLY

Referring to the assembly diagram below, arrange and sew nine rows of seven blocks each. (You'll have 28 leftover blocks.) Sew the rows together.

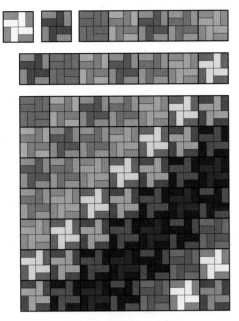

Assembly diagram

QUILTING AND FINISHING

Refer to "Quiltmaking Basics" on page 90 as needed for the following steps.

1. Layer, baste, and quilt. Catherine machine quilted three concentric circles in each block.

2. Bind the quilt with the 2½"-wide turquoise plaid strips.

PUT LEFTOVERS TO GOOD USE

Sew four of your extra blocks together to make the top for a matching stadium seat cushion. You have enough leftover blocks to make cushion tops for the whole family!

RUSSIAN SAGE

This captivating quilt vibrates with the colors of a circus. Fabrics from the Belle collection by Westminster Fibers give this throw an exotically contemporary look.

Designed by Gerri Robinson; machine quilted by Rebecca Segura of Zeffie's Quilts

Finished quilt size: 60½" x 60½"
Number of blocks and finished size: 9 Alabama Variation blocks, 18" x 18"

PLANNING

The use of a design wall or other large, flat surface is essential in arranging the patches for these blocks. Referring to the assembly diagram on page 45 and the quilt photos, lay out diagonal lines of fuchsia squares. Arrange the patches cut from the fat eighths to complete the outside edges of the outer blocks. Fill in the remaining spaces with the patches cut from the fat quarters.

FABRIC REQUIREMENTS

A fat eighth is a 9" x 20"–22" cut of fabric. A fat quarter is an 18" x 20"–22" cut of fabric, or a true quarter of a yard.

- Fuchsia-and-cream print (blocks, binding), 1½ yards
- 12 assorted bright prints (edges of outer blocks), 1 fat eighth *each*
- 12 assorted bright prints (remainder of blocks), 1 fat quarter *each*
- Charcoal-and-blue print (border), 1 yard
- Backing, 4 yards
- Batting, twin size

CUTTING

Fuchsia-and-cream print:

153 squares, 2½" x 2½"

8 binding strips, 2½" x 42"

12 assorted bright print fat eighths—cut from *each*:

3 squares, 2½" x 2½" (36 total)

2 rectangles, 2½" x 4½" (24 total)

3 strips, 2½" x 6½" (36 total)

12 assorted bright print fat quarters—cut from *each*:

6 squares, 2½" x 2½" (72 total)

4 rectangles, 2½" x 4½" (48 total)

6 strips, 2½" x 6½" (72 total)

Charcoal-and-blue print:

8 strips, 3½" x 42"

PIECING THE BLOCKS

1. Arrange the fabric pieces on a design surface (see "Planning" above). Using nine 2½" squares from the center of the first block on the design surface, make a nine-patch unit. Replace on the design surface. Repeat with the remaining block centers to make nine total nine-patch units.

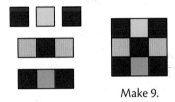

Make 9.

2. Use three fuchsia 2½" squares, two assorted 2½" x 4½" rectangles, and two matching assorted 2½" squares to make a block corner unit. Make four for each block (36 total), replacing each on the design surface as completed.

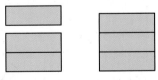

Make 36.

3. Sew three matching 2½" x 6½" strips together to make a block side unit. Make four for each block (36 total) and replace on the design surface.

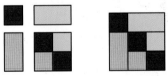

Make 36.

④ Sew the side units, corner units, and a block center together in three rows. Sew the rows together to make an Alabama Variation block. Make nine blocks total, replacing each on the design surface as it's completed.

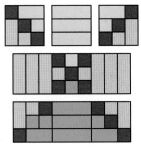 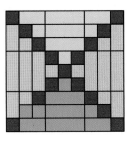

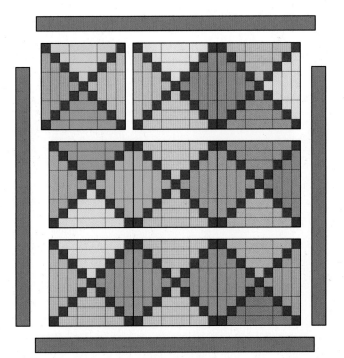

Make 9.

QUILT-TOP ASSEMBLY

Refer to the assembly diagram below for the following steps.

① Sew the blocks together in three rows of three blocks each. Sew the rows together.

② Stitch the charcoal-and-blue strips together end to end in pairs to make four long border strips. Sew two of the borders to the quilt sides; trim even with the top and bottom. Stitch the two remaining strips to the top and bottom of the quilt; trim even with the sides.

QUILTING AND FINISHING

Refer to "Quiltmaking Basics" on page 90 as needed for the following steps.

① Layer, baste, and quilt. Rebecca machine quilted with rainbow variegated thread in an allover floral meander.

② Bind with the 2½"-wide fuchsia-and-cream print strips.

Assembly diagram

COUNTRYSIDE STAR

Where does one block end and another begin? This delightful piecing puzzle is really quite simple to construct with easy-to-make blocks. Quick strip-piecing methods with short strips make easy work of the Strip-Pieced blocks. Choose subdued cream and green prints for the blocks and bolder greens for the leaves. The graceful appliqué nicely frames the bold stars in the quilt center. Use an accurate ¼" seam allowance for all the piecing so the various parts fit together well.

Designed by Ann Weber; machine quilted by Cheryl Kotecki
of Reems Creek Creative Quilting
Finished quilt size: 60½" x 72½"
Number of blocks and finished sizes: 28 Square-in-a-Square blocks, 6" x 6";
31 Strip-Pieced blocks, 6" x 6"; 4 Corner blocks, 9" x 9"

FABRIC REQUIREMENTS

- Assorted cream prints (piecing), 1½ yards *total*
- Assorted red prints (piecing), 1 yard *total*
- Assorted light green prints (Strip-Pieced blocks), 1⅝ yards *total*
- Cream print (border), 1⅞ yards
- Green-on-green print (stems), ⅜ yard
- Assorted dark pink prints (flowers), ⅝ yard *total*
- Assorted light pink prints (flowers), ⅜ yard *total*
- Assorted yellow prints (flower centers), ⅛ yard *total*
- Assorted medium green prints (leaves), ⅝ yard *total*
- Assorted blue prints (circles), ⅜ yard *total*
- Red-and-green print (binding), ¾ yard
- Backing (piece widthwise), 4 yards
- Batting, twin size
- Bias bar, ½" (optional)

CUTTING

Assorted cream prints—cut a *total* of:
 76 squares, 3⅞" x 3⅞"
 28 squares, 3½" x 3½"
 4 squares, 6½" x 6½"

Assorted red prints—cut a *total* of:
 76 squares, 3⅞" x 3⅞"

Assorted light green prints—cut a *total* of:
 52 strips, 2" x 20"

Cream print:
 4 strips, 6½" x 64", cut on the *lengthwise* grain

Green-on-green print:
 4 strips, 1½" x 30"
 4 strips, 1½" x 20"

Red-and-green print:
 7 binding strips, 2½" x 42"

PIECING THE BLOCKS

1. Draw a diagonal line on the wrong side of a cream 3⅞" square. Place the marked square on a red square, right sides together. Sew a ¼"-wide seam on each side of the marked line; cut apart on the marked line. Press open to make two pieced squares. Make 152 total.

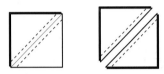

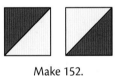

Make 152.

2. Join two pieced squares to make a flying-geese unit. Make 18 total. Sew together four pieced squares to make a Square-in-a-Square block. Make 28 total.

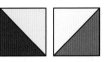

Make 18.

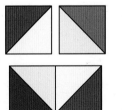

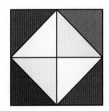

Make 28.

③ Sew together two cream 3½" squares to make a pieced rectangle. Make 10 total.

Make 10.

④ Sew together four assorted light green 2" x 20" strips. Make 13 total, varying the placement of the fabrics. Press the seam allowances as shown. Cut into 62 segments, 3½" wide. Join two segments to make a Strip-Pieced block. Make 31 blocks total. *Note:* When sewing two segments together, rotate one so the seam allowances are pressed in opposite directions. This will make them nest together when seaming.

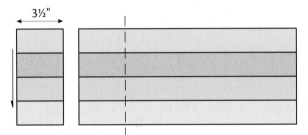

Make 13 strip sets.
Cut 62 segments.

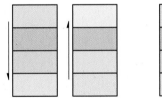

Make 31.

⑤ Watching orientation, use one cream 6½" square, two cream 3½" squares, a pieced square, and a flying-geese unit to make a Corner block. Make four total.

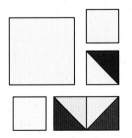

Make 4.

QUILT-TOP ASSEMBLY

Refer to the assembly diagram below for the following steps, watching the orientation of blocks and units throughout.

① For the top and bottom rows, first sew together three flying-geese units and two pieced rectangles, alternating them. Join three Strip-Pieced blocks and two Square-in-a-Square blocks. Sew the flying-geese strip to the top of the block strip. Add Corner blocks to the ends, watching orientation. Make two of these rows total.

② Watching placement and orientation carefully, stitch seven middle rows using flying-geese units, blocks, and pieced rectangles.

③ Sew the rows together, making sure to orient the top and bottom rows so that the flying-geese units point outward at each end of the quilt top.

④ Sew cream print 64" strips to the sides of the quilt; trim even with the top and bottom. Sew the remaining cream strips to the top and bottom of the quilt; trim even with the sides.

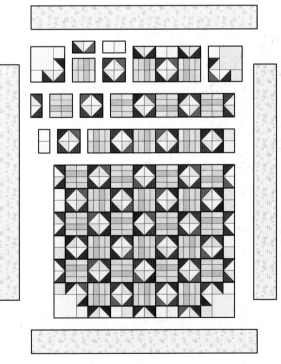

Assembly diagram

ADDING THE APPLIQUÉ

The appliqué patterns are on page 51. Appliqué patterns are printed without seam allowance.

① Prepare the following pieces for your favorite method of appliqué.

- **Large petal (A):** cut 8 sets of 4 matching large petals from assorted dark pink fabrics
- **Small petal (B):** cut 8 sets of 4 matching small petals from assorted light pink fabrics
- **Flower center (C):** cut 8 from assorted yellow fabrics; cut 72 from assorted blue fabrics
- **Leaf (D):** cut 40 from assorted medium green prints

② For the stems, fold a green-on-green print 30" strip in half lengthwise, wrong sides together. Stitch ½" from the folded edge. Trim the seam allowance to ⅛". Press the tube flat, centering the seam allowance on the back so the raw edges aren't visible from the front. Using a ½" bias bar makes pressing faster and easier. Repeat with the remaining green-on-green print 30" and 20" strips.

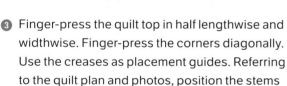

③ Finger-press the quilt top in half lengthwise and widthwise. Finger-press the corners diagonally. Use the creases as placement guides. Referring to the quilt plan and photos, position the stems and appliqué shapes A–D; appliqué in place.

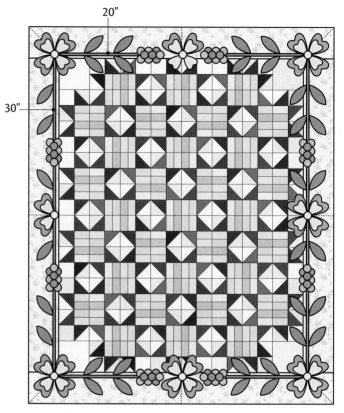

20"

30"

Quilt plan

QUILTING AND FINISHING

Refer to "Quiltmaking Basics" on page 90 as needed for the following steps.

① Layer, baste, and quilt. Cheryl machine quilted diagonal lines in the Strip-Pieced blocks. She added wavy lines in the red triangles and floral motifs in the cream patches of the Square-in-a-Square blocks. The appliqué was outline and echo quilted.

② Bind the quilt with the 2½"-wide red-and-green print strips.

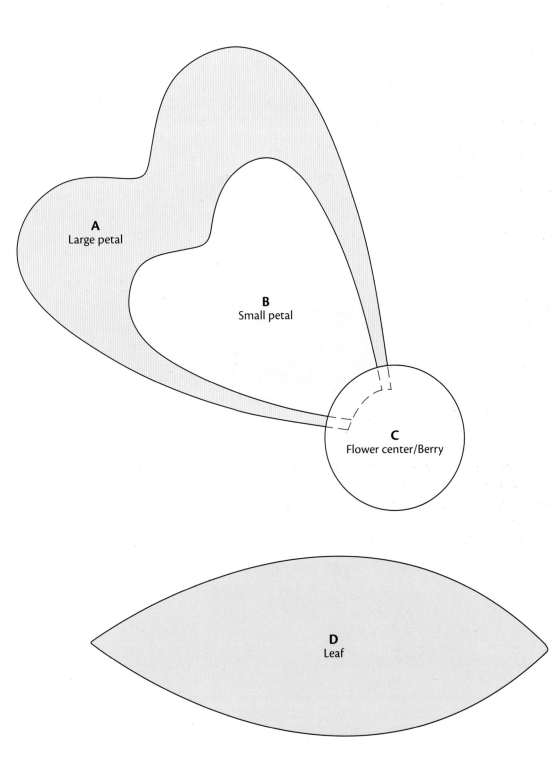

A
Large petal

B
Small petal

C
Flower center/Berry

D
Leaf

GARDEN STATE

This quilt is as refreshing as a cool breeze after a balmy April shower. Choose a variety of spring greens, plus orange for the inner border and appliqué. Toby cut some of the flowers from the orange inner-border fabric. You'll have sufficient fabric to do the same if you wish. Jumbo rickrack and buttons add whimsy to the scalloped border. If you have never bound curved edges, this is your chance to learn a new skill!

Designed by Toby Preston

Finished quilt size: 87" x 102"

This cheerful green, white, and orange quilt will add a burst of spring to a room. But don't be afraid to change up the color plan to make the most of your personal stash and to suit your own decor. Blue squares with golden flowers, purple squares with hot pink flowers, or a wildflower mix of colors could all work quite nicely.

FABRIC REQUIREMENTS

- Assorted green prints (squares, leaves), 2⅞–3¼ yards *total*
- Assorted cream prints (squares), 1¾–2⅛ yards *total*
- Orange print (inner border, binding), 1¾ yards
- Cream-and-green print (squares, scalloped border), 3¼ yards
- Assorted orange prints (flowers), 1–1¼ yards *total*
- Paper-backed fusible web, 3½ yards
- Backing (piece widthwise), 8 yards
- Batting, king size
- Green jumbo (¾") rickrack, 12 yards
- Green pearl cotton
- Assorted brown, gold, and green buttons (⅜"–¾"), 30–40
- See-through template plastic, 1 sheet
- Removable fabric marking pen
- Fabric glue (optional)

CUTTING

Appliqué patterns and border scallop template are on pages 56–59. Appliqué patterns D and E are printed without seam allowances for use with paper-backed fusible web.

Assorted green prints—cut a *total* of:
46 squares, 8" x 8"
30 *each* using leaf E and E reversed

Assorted cream prints—cut a *total* of:
35 squares, 8" x 8"

Orange print:
*1 square, 33" x 33" (for 2½"-wide bias-cut binding)
7 strips, 2½" x 42"
2 strips, 2½" x 42"; crosscut into 8 pieces, 2½" x 8"

Cream-and-green print:
**4 strips, 8" x 92", cut on the *lengthwise* grain
18 squares, 8" x 8"

Assorted orange prints—cut a *total* of:
30 using flower D

Cut first. Instructions for making continuous bias from a square are on page 95.
**Cut first.*

QUILT-TOP ASSEMBLY

Refer to the assembly diagram on page 54 for the following steps.

1. Sew five rows using four assorted green 8" squares and three assorted cream 8" squares each. Sew four rows using four cream 8" squares and three green 8" squares each. Sew the rows together, alternating them.

2. Sew three of the 2½" x 42" orange strips together end to end. From this long strip, cut two strips, 53" long. Sew them to the top and bottom of the quilt. In the same manner, sew the remaining 2½" x 42" orange strips together end to end and from this long strip, cut two strips, 72" long. Sew them to the quilt sides. Press.

3. Sew two pieced strips using four cream-and-green 8" squares and three green 8" squares each. Stitch an orange 8" strip to each end of the pieced strips. Sew these strips to the top and bottom of the quilt top, aligning the orange strips with the orange border.

4. Sew two pieced strips using five cream-and-green 8" squares and four green 8" squares each. Stitch an orange 8" strip and assorted cream 8" square to each end of each pieced strip. Sew these strips to the quilt sides, aligning the orange strips with the orange borders.

⑤ Sew cream-and-green 92" strips to opposite sides of the quilt top; trim the strips even with the top and bottom of the quilt. Sew the remaining cream-and-green strips to the top and bottom of the quilt and trim even with the sides.

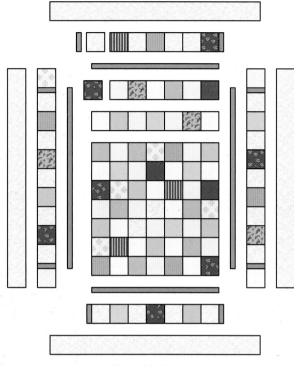

Assembly diagram

MARKING THE SCALLOPED EDGES

① Copy the scallop patterns (pages 56–59) and then trace them onto see-through plastic and cut them out to make templates for marking the scallops on the borders.

② Position the corner A/A reversed template on the corner of the quilt top and use removable marker to mark the fabric border along the curved edge of the template. Repeat on all four quilt corners.

③ Using the top/bottom B template, mark six scallops on the top border and six on the bottom border.

④ Using the side C template, mark seven scallops on each side border. Adjust the scallops as needed to fit the borders. *Do not* trim the edge of the scallops until the quilting has been completed.

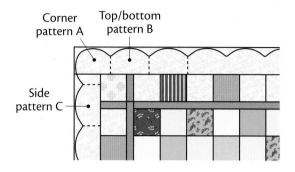

Corner pattern A

Top/bottom pattern B

Side pattern C

ADDING THE APPLIQUÉ

① Position the center of the rickrack 1½" inside the marked scallop line. Pin or use dots of fabric glue to hold the rickrack in place. Overlap the ends neatly, trimming as needed. Machine straight stitch through the center of the rickrack to secure.

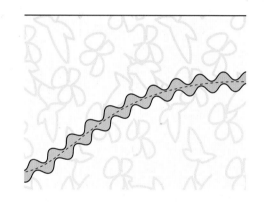

② Prepare the D, E, and E reversed appliqués for fusible appliqué. Referring to the quilt photograph on page 52, position the shapes on the border. Following the manufacturer's instructions, fuse in place. *Note:* Toby secured the appliqué during the quilting process. Do likewise, or finish the appliqué edges as you wish now.

QUILTING AND FINISHING

Refer to "Quiltmaking Basics" on page 90 as needed for the following steps.

1. Layer, baste, and quilt. Toby quilted the center squares with an overall continuous paisley motif. The inner border features a small leafy vine and a large continuous feather fills the pieced border. In the outer border, Toby quilted two echo lines outside of the rickrack and she filled the background with a meander. Quilted details in the appliqué include veins in the leaves (see pattern E/E reversed) and radiating lines in the flowers.

2. When the quilting is complete, check the marked scallops. If the quilting process has distorted them, repeat the marking process. Stitch along the marked scallop lines through all layers.

3. Make bias-cut binding. Fold the binding strip in half lengthwise, wrong sides together, and press. Align and pin the raw edges of the binding along the marked scalloped line on the quilt top and stitch ¼" from the raw edge of the binding. Ease rather than stretch the binding along the outer curves.

4. Trim the excess border/batting/backing even with the binding raw edge. Roll the binding to the back of the quilt and stitch in place, making a V-shape fold at the inner corners.

5. Using green pearl cotton, tack buttons to the flower centers. Toby stacked a small button on top of a larger one on several flowers.

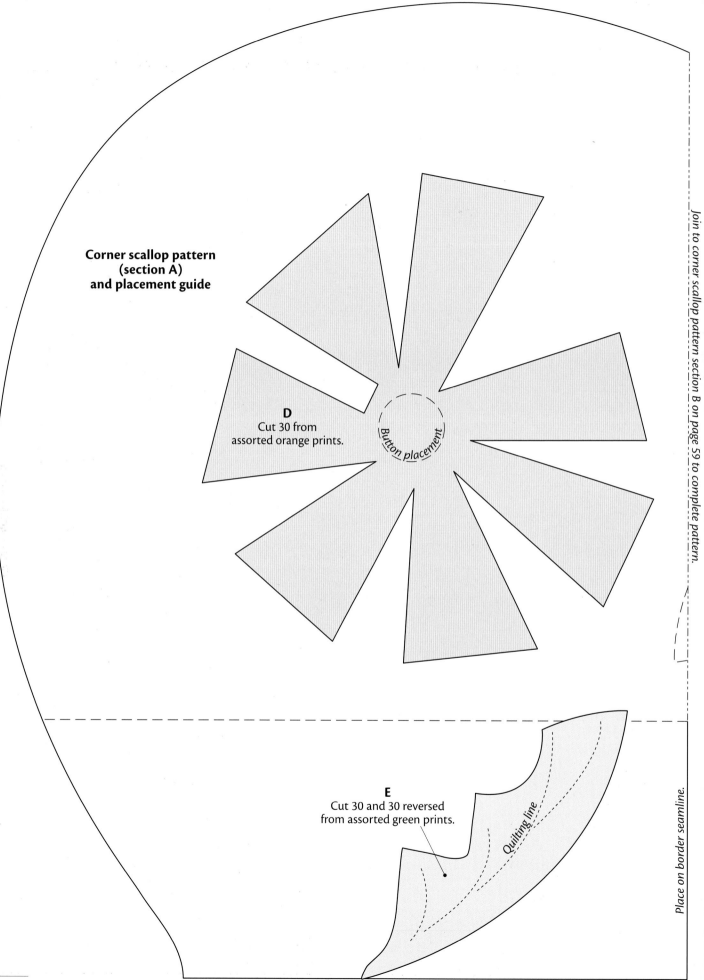

**Corner scallop pattern
(section A)
and placement guide**

Join to corner scallop pattern section B on page 59 to complete pattern.

D
Cut 30 from
assorted orange prints.

Button placement

E
Cut 30 and 30 reversed
from assorted green prints.

Quilting line

Place on border seamline.

Join to top/bottom scallop pattern section B on page 59 to complete pattern.

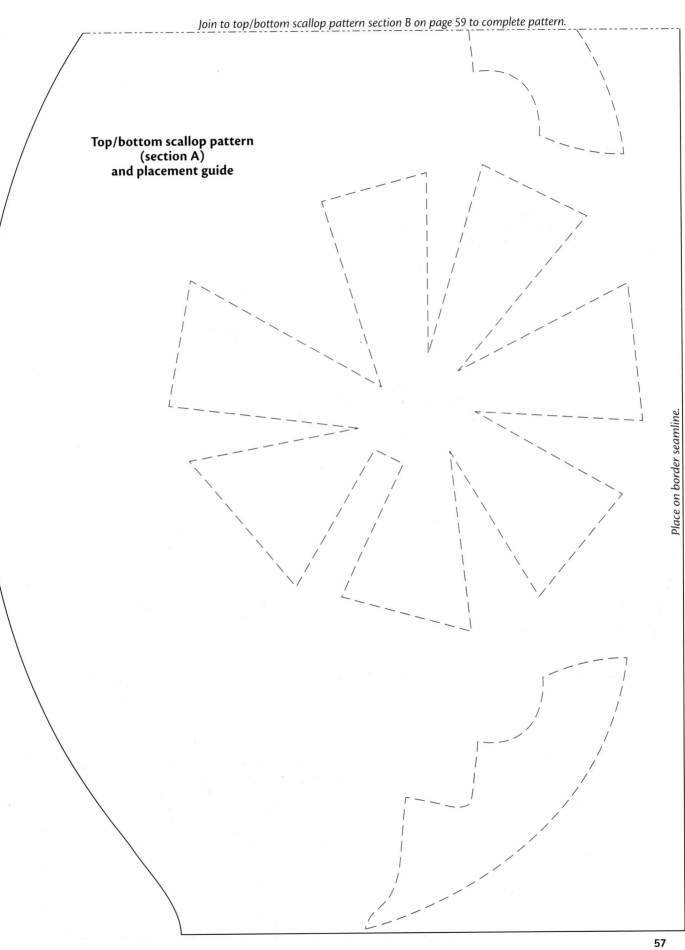

**Top/bottom scallop pattern
(section A)
and placement guide**

Place on border seamline.

Join to side scallop pattern section B on page 59 to complete pattern.

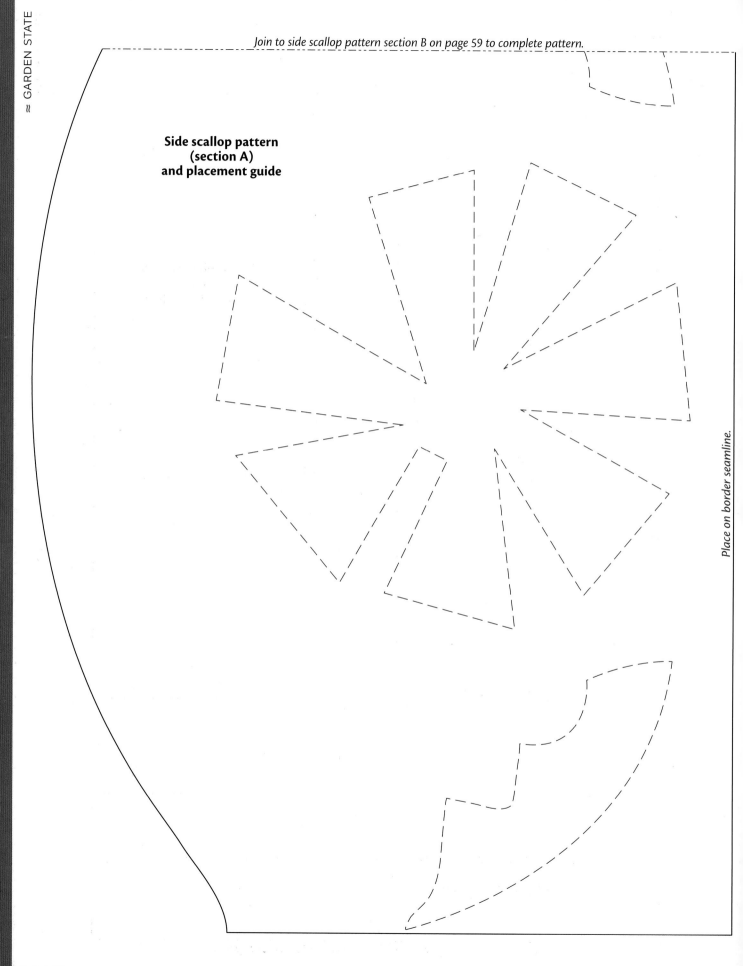

**Side scallop pattern
(section A)
and placement guide**

Place on border seamline.

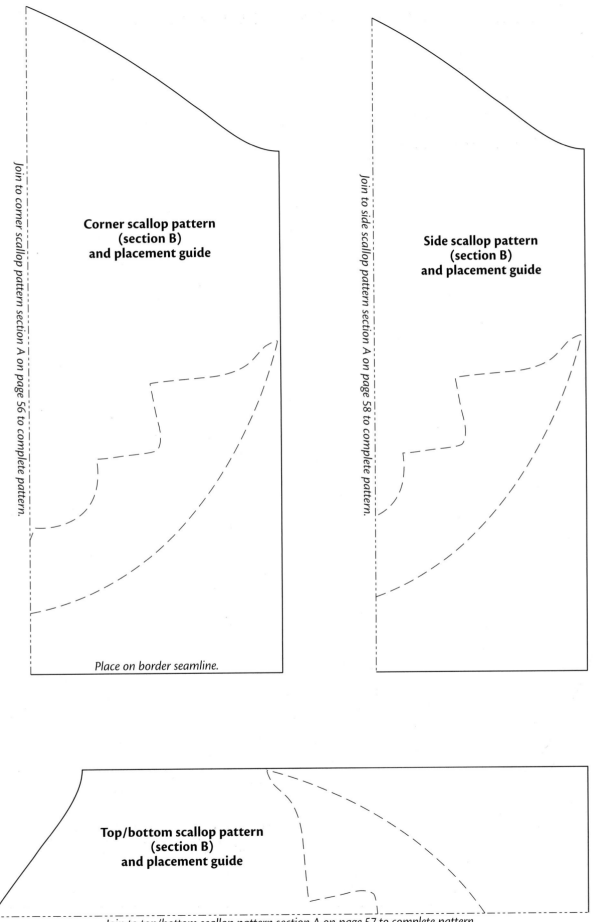

Join to corner scallop pattern section A on page 56 to complete pattern.

**Corner scallop pattern
(section B)
and placement guide**

Place on border seamline.

Join to side scallop pattern section A on page 58 to complete pattern.

**Side scallop pattern
(section B)
and placement guide**

**Top/bottom scallop pattern
(section B)
and placement guide**

Join to top/bottom scallop pattern section A on page 57 to complete pattern.

ANGEL FOOD

She's always there, picks her loved ones up when they fall, and watches over them like a guardian angel. Your favorite mom deserves a heavenly treat, so show how much you appreciate her with this sweet, soft lap-size quilt.

Designed by Rebecca LoGiudice; machine quilted by Leslie Armando of Distinctive Quilting

Finished quilt size: 64½" x 64½"
Number of blocks and finished size: 36 Pieced blocks, 8½" x 8½"

PLANNING

Rebecca designed this charming quilt using a Layer Cake of 40 fabric squares, 10" x 10", purchased at her local quilt shop, plus fabric from her stash. Although the featured quilt is slightly scrappier, our instructions are written for using just forty 10" squares to piece the blocks. Use your favorite Layer Cake and add pleasing fabrics for borders and binding.

FABRIC REQUIREMENTS

- Assorted prints (blocks), 40 squares, 10" x 10"
- Green print #1 (inner border), 1 fat quarter
- Green print #2 (inner border), ⅜ yard
- Blue floral (outer border), 2 yards
- Green print #3 (binding), ⅞ yard
- Backing, 4¼ yards
- Batting, twin size
- Square acrylic ruler, 9" (or larger)

CUTTING

36 assorted print squares—use the cutting diagram below to cut from *each*:
    1 strip, 3½" x 10"
    1 rectangle, 3½" x 6½"
    1 square, 6½" x 6½"

4 remaining assorted print squares—cut *9 sets* of:
    2 matching squares, 3" x 3" (18 squares total)

Green print #1:
    8 strips, 1½" x 10"

Green print #2:
    4 strips, 1½" x 38½"

Blue floral:
    2 strips, 6" x 58", cut on the *lengthwise* grain
    2 strips, 6" x 68", cut on the *lengthwise* grain

Green print #3:
    8 binding strips, 2½" x 42"

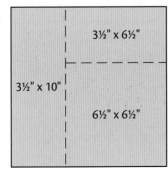

Cutting diagram

PIECING THE BLOCKS

1. Using three different prints for each block, sew a 3½" x 6½" rectangle to a 6½" square; add a 3½" x 10" strip to either side to make a Pieced block. Trim the block to 9" x 9" using a square acrylic ruler. Make 36 total.

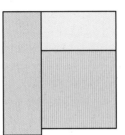 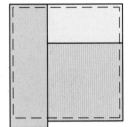

Trim to 9" square.

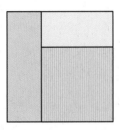

Make 36.

EASY TRIMMING

For easy, uniform trimming of blocks, align the 3" line on your ruler with each seam and trim. Then trim the remaining block sides to 9".

2. Referring to the assembly diagram on page 63, position six rows of six blocks each in a pleasing arrangement. Then plan the placement of the matching sets of 3" squares for each group of four blocks. Draw a diagonal line on the wrong side of an assorted 3" square. Place a marked square on a pieced block as shown, right sides together and

aligning the raw edges. Sew on the marked line; trim away and discard the excess fabric. Press open. Repeat the process for 18 total pieced blocks.

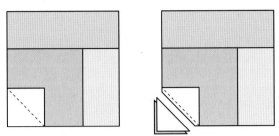

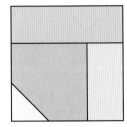

Make 18.

3 Sew two rows of two blocks each, watching the position of the pieced triangles on the block corners. Sew the rows together to make a large pieced square. Make nine total.

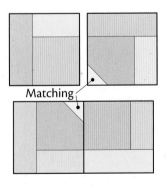

Matching

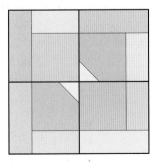

Make 9.

QUILT-TOP ASSEMBLY

Refer to the assembly diagram below for the following steps.

1 Sew three rows of three large pieced squares each. Sew the rows together to make the quilt center.

2 Stitch 10" green #1 strips to both ends of the 38½" green #2 strips to make four pieced strips. Finger-press the quilt center in half both lengthwise and widthwise. Finger-press the pieced strips in half. Sew the pieced strips to the sides of the quilt center, matching the fold lines. Trim the strips even with the quilt top and bottom. Repeat to add the remaining pieced strips to the top and bottom of the quilt; trim strips even with the sides.

3 Sew the blue 58" strips to the quilt sides; trim even. Stitch the remaining blue strips to the top and bottom of the quilt; trim even.

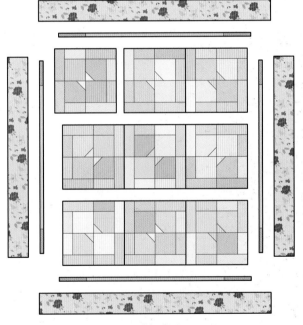

Assembly diagram

QUILTING AND FINISHING

Refer to "Quiltmaking Basics" on page 90 as needed for the following steps.

1 Layer, baste, and quilt. Leslie machine quilted an allover swirling meander.

2 Bind the quilt with the 2½"-wide green #3 strips.

ANTIQUE BUTTON BAZAAR

So striking, so easy, so unique! Gather those batiks that you've been saving and sew a fast, easy quilt. With or without button embellishment, the graphic power and understated color scheme of this quilt will delight any sophisticated snuggler.

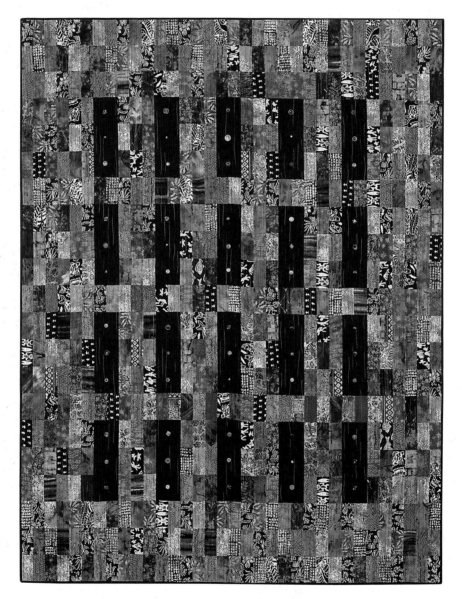

Designed by Joyce Robinson
Finished quilt size: 85½" x 105½"

The simplicity of this design can lend itself to many different color ideas and finished looks. Here the finished quilt has an overall muted appearance, but if your stash is overflowing with 1930s prints, why not use those up and replace the black solid with a 1930s solid green or yellow? Or if bright colors are your favorites, use a mix of those with the large black rectangles. If you use a lighter color for the large rectangles, you could even turn this project into a signature quilt where everyone signs her name in the big rectangles.

FABRIC REQUIREMENTS

- Assorted black-and-white, blue, and brown batiks, 7¼–8 yards *total*
- Black solid (piecing, binding), 2½ yards
- Backing (pieced widthwise), 8 yards
- Batting, king size
- 60 buttons in assorted sizes and colors

CUTTING

Assorted batiks—cut a *total* of:
594 rectangles, 3" x 5½"

Black solid:
20 strips, 5½" x 15½"
10 binding strips, 2½" x 42"

PIECING THE STRIPS

1. Arrange and sew a single vertical strip using 21 assorted batik 3" x 5½" rectangles, sewing the rectangles together along their 3" edges. Make 24 total pieced strips.

2. Sew two assorted batik rectangles together to make a double segment. Make 45 total. Set 15 aside.

Make 45.

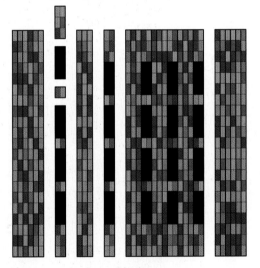

Make 24.

3. Sew the remaining 30 double segments together in sets of three to make 10 pieced rectangles.

Make 10.

QUILT-TOP ASSEMBLY

1. Referring to the assembly diagram below, arrange and sew five vertical strips using two pieced rectangles, four black solid strips, and three double segments each.

2. Stitch three single vertical strips (made in step 1 of "Piecing the Strips") together to make a triple strip. Make four.

3. Sew the rows from steps 1 and 2 together, alternating them, for the quilt center.

4. Stitch the remaining 12 single vertical strips together in two panels of six strips each. Sew these panels to the sides of the quilt center.

Assembly diagram

QUILTING AND FINISHING

Refer to "Quiltmaking Basics" on page 90 as needed for the following steps.

1. Layer, baste, and quilt. Joyce machine quilted vertical wavy lines the length of the quilt.

2. Bind the quilt with the 2½"-wide black solid strips.

3. Tack three assorted buttons to each black strip, centering them vertically.

TRADE WINDS

Joyce made her scrap quilt glow with fall colors. Whether you're a preplanner who likes to sew one block at a time, or the type to pull fabrics from your stash and start cutting, this project is for you. It's a great project for block exchanges, too.

Designed by Joyce Stewart; machine quilted by Virginia Gore

Finished quilt size: 87½" x 95½"
Number of blocks and finished size: 90 Shadow Box Variation blocks, 8" x 8"

Find a favorite print to use for the border, and then head to your stash to pull coordinating colors for the blocks. Choose a variety of light, medium, and dark prints for the centers and first two triangle rounds of the blocks, followed by a round of dark triangles. Finish off the block by adding greens and golds for the last triangles, complementing the outer-border fabric.

FABRIC REQUIREMENTS

- Assorted light, medium, and dark prints (block centers, rounds 1 and 2), 2⅝–3 yards *total*
- Assorted dark brown, red, and rust prints (round 3), 1⅛–1⅜ yards *total*
- Assorted dark green and blue prints (round 3), 1⅛–1⅜ yards total
- Assorted medium green prints (round 4), 1⅞–2¼ yards *total*
- Assorted medium yellow and gold prints (round 4), 1⅞–2¼ yards *total*
- Red mottled print (inner border, binding), 1⅜ yards
- Green-and-gold leaf print (outer border), 2¾ yards
- Backing (pieced widthwise), 8⅛ yards
- Batting, king size

CUTTING

Assorted light, medium, and dark prints:

90 sets of 2 matching squares, 2⅜" x 2⅜"; cut in half diagonally to make 4 half-square triangles (360 total)

90 sets of 2 matching squares, 2⅞" x 2⅞"; cut in half diagonally to make 4 half-square triangles (360 total)

90 squares, 2½" x 2½"

Assorted dark brown, red, and rust prints—cut a *total* of:

90 squares, 3¾" x 3¾"; cut in half diagonally to make 180 half-square triangles

Assorted dark green and blue prints—cut a *total* of:

90 squares, 3¾" x 3¾"; cut in half diagonally to make 180 half-square triangles

Assorted medium green prints—cut a *total* of:

90 squares, 4⅞" x 4⅞"; cut in half diagonally to make 180 half-square triangles

Assorted medium yellow and gold prints—cut a *total* of:

90 squares, 4⅞" x 4⅞"; cut in half diagonally to make 180 half-square triangles

Red mottled print:

9 strips, 1½" x 42"

10 binding strips, 2½" x 42"

Green-and-gold leaf print:

4 strips, 7" x 92", cut on the *lengthwise* grain

PIECING THE BLOCKS

1. Sew assorted matching 2⅜" half-square triangles to all four sides of an assorted 2½" square to make a pieced square as shown. Trim to 3⅜" square if necessary. Next, sew assorted matching 2⅞" half-square triangles to the pieced square.

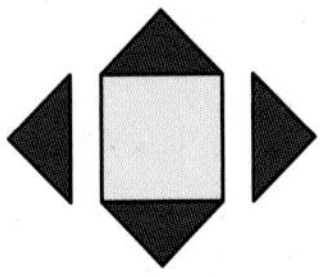

2. Stitch assorted matching sets of dark brown, red, or rust and dark green or blue 3¾" half-square triangles to the sides of the pieced square.

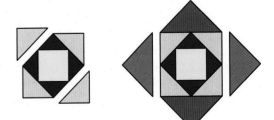

❸ Sew assorted matching sets of medium green and medium yellow or gold 4⅞" half-square triangles to the sides to make a Shadow Box Variation block. Make 90 total.

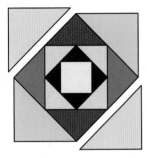 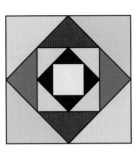

Make 90.

QUILT-TOP ASSEMBLY

Refer to the assembly diagram below and the quilt photos for the following steps.

❶ Sew 10 rows of nine blocks each, watching the positions of the yellow and green outer triangles. Stitch the rows together. Press.

❷ Sew the red 1½"-wide strips together end to end to make one long strip. From this strip, cut four inner-border strips, 84" long. Sew the strips to the quilt sides; trim even with the top and bottom of the quilt. Stitch the remaining red strips to the top and bottom of the quilt and trim even with the sides.

❸ Sew green-and-gold 92" strips to the quilt sides; trim even with the top and bottom of the quilt. Stitch the remaining green-and-gold strips to the top and bottom of the quilt; trim even with the sides.

QUILTING AND FINISHING

Refer to "Quiltmaking Basics" on page 90 as needed for the following steps.

❶ Layer, baste, and quilt. Virginia machine quilted a large swirling feather meander in the quilt center. A curving line is centered in the inner-border strips and a continuous leaf-and-stem pattern fills the outer border.

❷ Bind the quilt with the 2½"-wide red mottled strips.

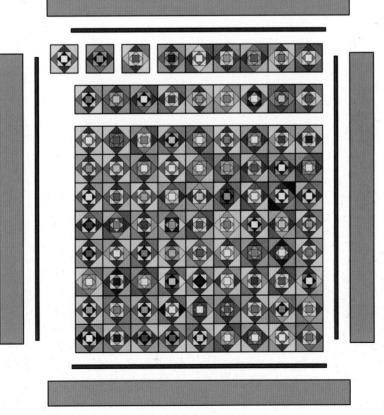

Assembly diagram

PATCHWORK PRESERVES

Anything goes in this one-patch quilt. Combine big, noisy prints with quiet little calicoes, and throw in a few solid colors for flair; variations in color and value really bring the quilt to life. For a true one-patch charm quilt, cut each patch from a different fabric. A scrap exchange with your quilting friends can provide a large variety of fabrics. The quilt shown was an antique hand-pieced top that Susan appliquéd to her chosen border. If you hand piece, this is a super carry-along project.

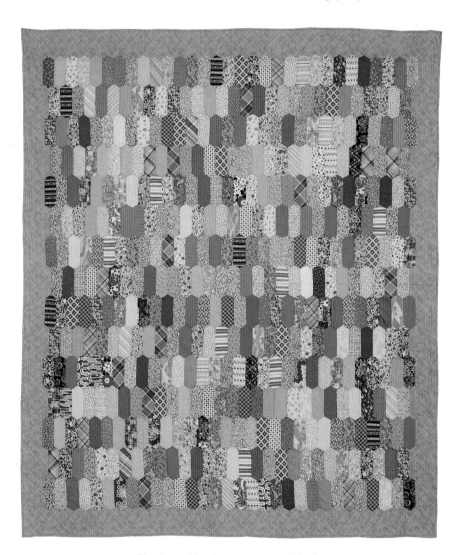

Designed by Susan Purney Mark

Finished quilt size: 79¼" x 94½"

To cut patches, trace the pattern for template A on page 73 onto template plastic, including grain line and match points. Cut out the template on the marked lines and make holes at the match points using a stiletto or large needle. Place the plastic template on the wrong side of the fabric (watching the grain line), mark around the edges, cut out the patch, and transfer the match points to the fabric wrong side.

We suggest you wash the muslin before cutting to allow for shrinkage.

FABRIC REQUIREMENTS

- Assorted prints and solids (quilt center), 8–8½ yards *total*
- Muslin (background), 4½ yards*
- Blue plaid (border, binding), ⅜ yards
- Backing (piece widthwise), 7½ yards
- Batting, queen size
- Template plastic, 3" x 7" piece

Yardage based on at least 34" of usable width.

CUTTING INSTRUCTIONS

Assorted prints and solids—cut a *total* of:

458 using template A

Muslin:

2 strips, 31" x 78", cut on the *lengthwise* grain

Blue plaid:

*9 binding strips, 2½" x 42"

4 strips, 10" x 84", cut on the *lengthwise* grain

Cut first.

PIECING THE QUILT CENTER

1. Starting and stopping at the match points, stitch two A patches right sides together along one long edge.

2. Repeat to stitch a total of 31 A patches together to make a long row. Make eight total. Stitch 30 A patches together to make a short row. Make seven total.

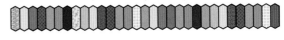

Long row.
Make 8.

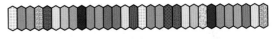

Short row.
Make 7.

3. Aligning raw edges and pivoting at every match point, sew the long and short rows together, alternating them, to make the quilt center. Press all seam allowances to one side. Press ¼" under on the outer edges of the quilt center.

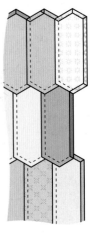

PIECING THE BACKGROUND

1. Join the two muslin 31" x 78" strips along one long edge. Sew two blue plaid 84" strips to the sides of the muslin base; trim the strips even with the top and bottom of the muslin.

❷ Stitch the remaining blue plaid strips to the top and bottom of the muslin base; trim them even with the sides to complete the base with borders.

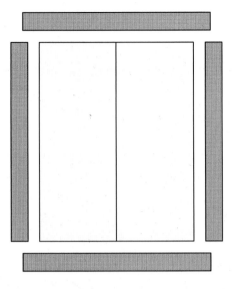

QUILT-TOP ASSEMBLY

❶ Center the pieced quilt center on the muslin base, right sides up. Smooth out the layers so that they are flat and the inside edge of the blue border lies completely under the pressed patch edges; no muslin should be showing.

❷ Pin the pressed patch edges to the blue plaid border. Appliqué by hand or machine. Cut away the excess background beneath the patches if desired, leaving ¼" seam allowances.

❸ Trim the edges of the border even, trimming the top and bottom edges 4¾" from the points of the patches and side edges 4¾" from the outermost patches.

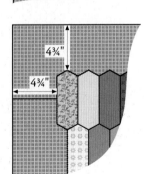

4¾"

4¾"

QUILTING AND FINISHING

Refer to "Quiltmaking Basics" on page 90 as needed for the following steps.

❶ Layer, baste, and quilt. Susan hand quilted large flower motifs in the pieced center and added machine quilting in the border that echoes the patch edges.

❷ Bind the quilt with the 2½"-wide blue plaid strips.

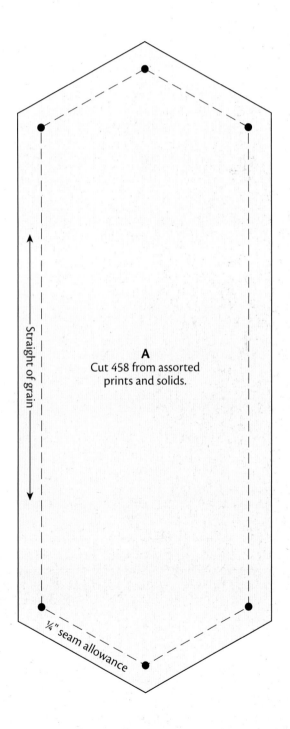

Straight of grain

A
Cut 458 from assorted prints and solids.

¼" seam allowance

APPLE CIDER

If you'd love to piece a bed-sized quilt this season, but are on a fabric budget, dip into your quilter's equity—your stash! Scrap quilts let you create with little or no investment in fabric. And if all your chosen prints have the same style or come from one designer, like our featured quilt, your results will have the unified look of a collection quilt, with no cash outlay!

Designed by Dolores Smith and Sarah Maxwell; machine quilted by Connie Gresham

Finished quilt size: 100½" x 100½"
**Number of blocks and finished size: All blocks are 10" x 10"; 13 of block A,
8 each of blocks B and B reversed (BR), 24 of block C, 12 of block D, and 16 of block E**

PLANNING

This appealing quilt looks complicated, but you'll be amazed how quickly it goes together. Made up of five simple block patterns, this scrap quilt is truly fun and easy to make. Many of the blocks are made using matching triangles. As you cut the pieces, keep matching sets of squares and triangles pinned together to speed the process and keep things organized. If you prefer a more random design, you can mix and match the cut pieces.

Note that four C blocks with matching black 5⅞" half-square triangles were positioned around the A block in the center of the quilt to form a cohesive star. Do likewise if you wish.

Be sure to sew with an accurate ¼" seam allowance so the pieced border will fit properly.

FABRIC REQUIREMENTS

- Assorted beige and tan prints, 4¼–4¾ yards *total*
- Assorted red prints, 1⅜–1⅝ yards *total*
- Assorted purple prints, 1⅛–1⅜ yards *total*
- Assorted black prints, 2–2¼ yards *total*
- Assorted green prints, 1⅛–1⅜ yards *total*
- Assorted light brown prints, 1⅝–1⅞ yards *total*
- Assorted blue prints, ¾–1 yard *total*
- Green print (border), 1¾ yards
- Black small floral (binding), 1⅛ yards
- Backing, 9¼ yards
- Batting, king size

CUTTING

Assorted beige and tan prints—cut *84 sets* of:
2 matching squares, 3" x 3" (168 total)

Assorted beige and tan prints—cut a *total* of:
164 squares, 3⅜" x 3⅜"; cut in half diagonally to make 328 half-square triangles
32 squares, 5⅞" x 5⅞"; cut in half diagonally to make 64 half-square triangles
16 squares, 5½" x 5½"

Assorted red prints—cut a *total* of:
132 squares, 3⅜" x 3⅜"; cut in half diagonally to make 264 half-square triangles

Assorted purple prints—cut a *total* of:
80 squares, 3" x 3"
24 squares, 3⅜" x 3⅜"; cut in half diagonally to make 48 half-square triangles

Assorted black prints—cut a *total* of:
52 squares, 5⅞" x 5⅞"; cut in half diagonally to make 104 half-square triangles
24 squares, 3⅜" x 3⅜"; cut in half diagonally to make 48 half-square triangles

Assorted green prints—cut a *total* of:
32 squares, 5⅞" x 5⅞"; cut in half diagonally to make 64 half-square triangles

Assorted light brown prints—cut *80 sets* of:
2 matching squares, 3⅜" x 3⅜"; cut in half diagonally to make 4 half-square triangles (320 total)

Assorted blue prints—cut *32 sets* of:
2 matching squares, 3⅜" x 3⅜"; cut in half diagonally to make 4 half-square triangles (128 total)

Green print:
*8 strips, 5½" x 30½"
12 squares, 5⅞" x 5⅞"; cut in half diagonally to make 24 half-square triangles
4 squares, 5½" x 5½"

Black small floral:
11 binding strips, 2½" x 42"
Cut first.

PIECING THE BLOCKS

Block A

1 Sew assorted red and assorted beige 3⅜" triangles together in pairs to make pieced squares. Make them in sets of two matching pieced squares; make a total of 52 sets (104 total pieced squares).

Make 52 sets of
2 matching units.

2 Using two matching pieced squares and two matching beige 3" squares, assemble the pieces in a four-patch arrangement. Make 52.

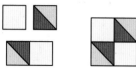

Make 52.

3 Assemble block A using two sets of four-patch units, arranging the units so that the matching units are diagonally opposite one another as shown. Repeat to make a total of 13 of block A.

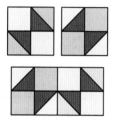

Block A.
Make 13.

Blocks B, B Reversed, and C

These blocks are similar and made from the same units, so pay careful attention to the unit arrangement as you complete the blocks.

1 Sew two matching beige 3⅜" triangles to adjacent sides of 3" purple squares. Make 80 total.

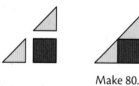

Make 80.

2 Sew a black 5⅞" triangle to the step 1 units. Make 80.

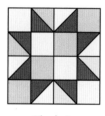

Make 80.

3 Sew assorted beige 5⅞" triangles to assorted green 5⅞" triangles to make 64 pieced squares.

Make 64.

4 To make block B, sew together two units from step 2, one pieced square from step 3, and one beige 5½" square as shown. Make eight of block B. Block B reversed uses the same pieces, but the step 2 units are on the opposite side of the block. Make eight of block B reversed. Pay close attention to the direction of the triangles within the block layout.

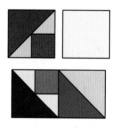

Block B.
Make 8.

Block B reversed.
Make 8.

5 To make block C, join two units from step 2 and two pieced squares from step 3 as shown. Make 24 of block C.

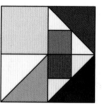

Block C.
Make 24.

Block D

1 Sew the 3⅜" purple, black, and red triangles to light brown 3⅜" triangles. Make 48 purple and 48 black pieced squares. Make 48 sets of matching red pieced squares.

Make 48. Make 48. Make 48 sets of 2 matching units.

2 Sew a purple, black, and two red pieced squares together as shown to make 48 units.

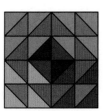

Make 48.

3 Sew together four units from step 2 with all the colored triangles pointing toward the block center to complete block D. Repeat to make a total of 12 of block D.

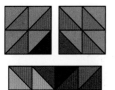

Block D.
Make 12.

Block E

1 Sew red 3⅜" and light brown 3⅜" triangles together to make pieced squares. Make 32 sets of two matching pieced squares. Repeat to make 32 sets of four matching pieced squares using the assorted blue and assorted light brown 3⅜" triangles.

Make 32 sets of 2 matching units. Make 32 sets of 4 matching units.

2 Referring to step 2 of block A on page 76, sew the red/beige units from step 1 together with beige 3" squares to make 32 units.

Make 32.

3 Sew the blue/light brown pieced squares from step 1 together with the blue triangles pointing in the same direction as shown. Make 32 units.

Make 32.

4 Sew two red units and two blue units together as shown to complete block E. Repeat to make a total of 16 of block E.

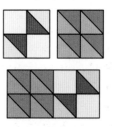 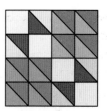

Block E.
Make 16.

PIECING THE BORDER STAR POINTS

1 Sew an assorted black 5⅞" triangle to a green print triangle to make a pieced square. Make 24 total.

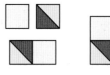

Make 24.

2 Sew two pieced squares together to make a pieced rectangle for border star points. Make 12 total.

Make 12.

QUILT-TOP ASSEMBLY

Refer to the assembly diagram below for the following steps.

1 Sew nine rows of nine blocks each, watching block placement and orientation. Stitch the rows together.

2 To piece the borders, sew strips using three pieced rectangles alternating with two green 5½" x 30½" strips. Make four total. Sew two of the pieced strips to the sides of the quilt. Stitch green 5½" squares to the ends of the remaining pieced strips, and then sew the strips to the top and bottom of the quilt.

QUILTING AND FINISHING

Refer to "Quiltmaking Basics" on page 90 as needed for the following steps.

1 Layer, baste, and quilt. Connie machine quilted an allover meander of flowers, leaves, vines, and stems.

2 Bind the quilt with the 2½"-wide black small floral strips.

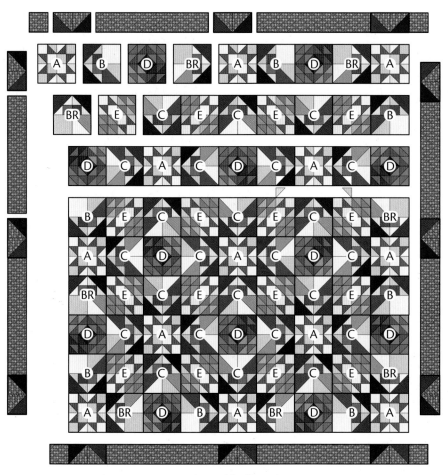

Assembly diagram

PICK A PUMPKIN

Treat a good neighbor to this celebration of autumn's bounty. It's the perfect thank-you for shared garden produce, homemade baked goods, or helpful favors. And the simple fused appliqué and easy-to-piece blocks leave plenty of time for visiting across the fence or on the porch.

Designed by Marianne Zenero Harwood

Finished quilt size: 38" x 43"
Number of blocks and finished sizes: 21 appliquéd blocks, various sizes;
4 Four Patch Variation blocks, 5" x 5"

If you love to do wool appliqué, this project would be perfect not only for using up some plaid and print cotton fabric scraps for the block backgrounds, but also for incorporating bits and pieces of wool, too. The pumpkins, leaves, and stars would all look great as wool appliqués, or mix it up and use what you have—a bit of wool here, some cotton appliqués there.

FABRIC REQUIREMENTS

- Red mottled print (leaves, middle border), ⅝ yard
- Green plaid (small stars, background, outer border, binding), 1⅜ yards
- Assorted orange prints (pumpkins, piecing), ½–¾ yard *total*
- 2 assorted green mottled prints (stems, piecing), 8" x 10" piece *each*
- Assorted gold, brown, and black prints (pumpkin details), ¼ yard *total*
- Purple print (leaves, background), 13" x 13" piece
- Cream-and-gold mottled print (leaves, piecing), 11" x 12" piece
- Brown-and-cream plaid (large stars, background), 12" x 12" piece
- Dark red print (background), 18" x 20" piece
- Cream print (background, piecing, inner border), ⅝ yard
- Dark gold plaid (background), 8" x 13" piece
- Backing, 2⅞ yards
- Batting, crib size
- Paper-backed fusible web, 2 yards
- Pumpkin and star buttons, 7 assorted
- Fine-tip brown permanent pen

CUTTING

Appliqué patterns are on pages 83–89 and are printed reversed and without seam allowances to use with paper-backed fusible web.

Red mottled print:
    *4 strips, 1½" x 42"

Green plaid:
    *5 binding strips, 2½" x 42"
    *5 strips, 2¾" x 42"
    2 squares, 10½" x 10½"
    2 squares, 5½" x 5½"
    4 squares, 2¾" x 2¾"

Assorted orange prints—cut a *total* of:
    4 squares, 2¾" x 2¾"

2 assorted green mottled prints—cut from *each*:
    2 strips, 1" x 5" (4 total)
    2 strips, 1" x 5½" (4 total)

Purple print, brown-and-cream plaid, and dark gold plaid—cut from *each*:
    2 squares, 5½" x 5½" (6 total)

Cream-and-gold mottled print:
    4 squares, 2¾" x 2¾"

Dark red print:
    4 strips, 3" x 10½"
    4 squares, 5½" x 5½"

Cream print:
    *4 strips, 1" x 42"
    *1 rectangle, 10½" x 15½"
    2 squares, 10½" x 10½"
    4 squares, 2¾" x 2¾"

Cut first.

MAKING THE BLOCKS

1. Trace all appliqué patterns on the paper side of paper-backed fusible web. Cut apart, leaving a small margin beyond the drawn lines. Following the manufacturer's instructions, fuse the shapes to the wrong side of the appropriate fabrics; cut out the appliqués on the drawn lines.

❷ Finger-press the background squares, strips, and rectangles in half both lengthwise and widthwise; use the folds as placement guides. Referring to the placement guides below and the quilt photos, position the appliqués on the background fabrics. Following the manufacturer's instructions, fuse in place.

Make 2.

Make 4.

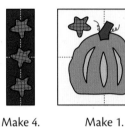

Make 1.

Make 2.

Make 2.

Make 2.

Make 2.

Make 2.

Make 2.

Make 1.

Make 1.

Appliqué block placement guides

❸ Secure the appliqué edges using machine or hand blanket stitch. Using a brown fine-tip permanent pen, draw a curlicue detail on the four large pumpkins (see the appliqué patterns for placement). Alternately, you could hand embroider the details.

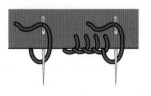

❹ Make a Four Patch Variation block using cream, orange mottled, green plaid, and cream-and-gold 2¾" squares as shown. Make four total. *Note:* For one of the blocks, Marianne rearranged the color placement of the squares. Do likewise if you wish.

Sew a green mottled 1" x 5" strip to one side of the Four Patch Variation blocks, paying careful attention to the color placement as shown. Then sew a 1" x 5½" green mottled strip to the adjacent side of each block.

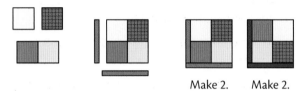

Make 2. Make 2.

QUILT-TOP ASSEMBLY

This wall hanging looks complex, but the quilt center is broken into three sections for easy assembly.

❶ Arrange and sew the three individual sections in horizontal rows. Sew the rows together.

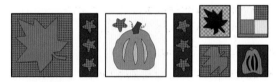

Section 1

Section 2

Section 3

❷ Referring to the assembly diagram on page 82, sew cream 1" x 42" strips to the quilt sides; trim them even with the top and bottom of the quilt. Stitch the remaining cream strips to the top and bottom of the quilt; trim even with the sides.

❸ Repeat using red mottled 1½" x 42" strips for the middle border.

④ For the outer border, sew two of the green plaid 2¾" strips to the quilt sides and trim even. Sew the remaining three green plaid 2¾" strips together end to end and cut into two borders, 46" long. Sew these strips to the top and bottom of the quilt; trim even.

Assembly diagram

QUILTING AND FINISHING

Refer to "Quiltmaking Basics" on page 90 as needed for the following steps.

① Layer, baste, and quilt. Marianne machine quilted the appliqué and borders in the ditch, and then added detail lines on the leaves. The background and outer border are filled with a meander.

② Bind the quilt with the 2½"-wide green plaid strips.

③ Tack buttons to the pieced blocks and on the large pumpkin stars.

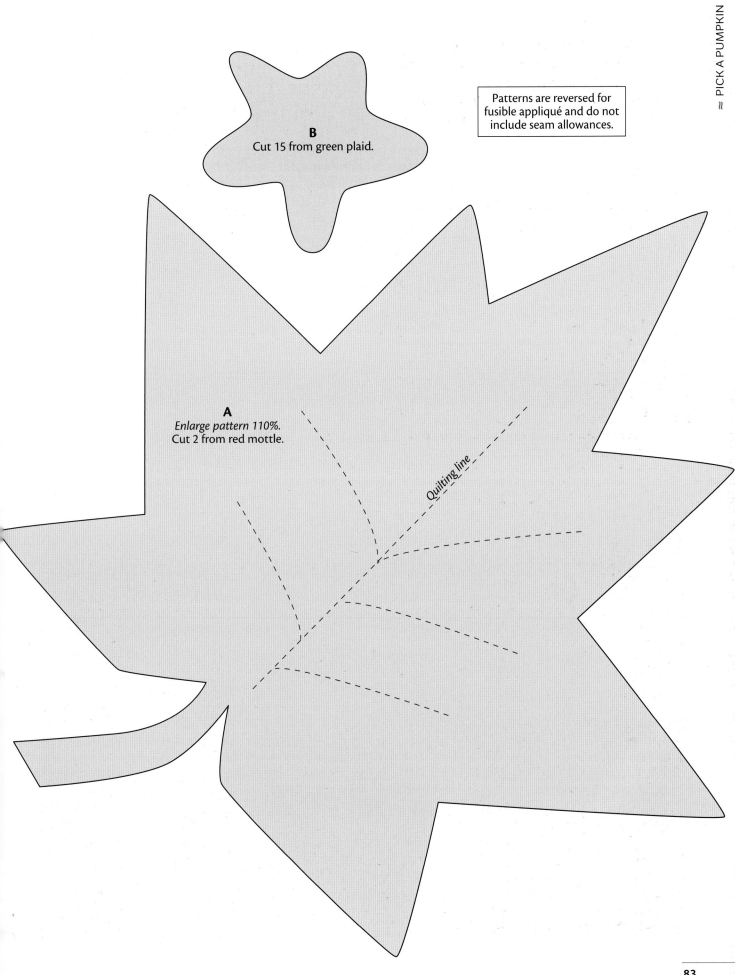

B
Cut 15 from green plaid.

Patterns are reversed for
fusible appliqué and do not
include seam allowances.

A
Enlarge pattern 110%.
Cut 2 from red mottle.

Quilting line

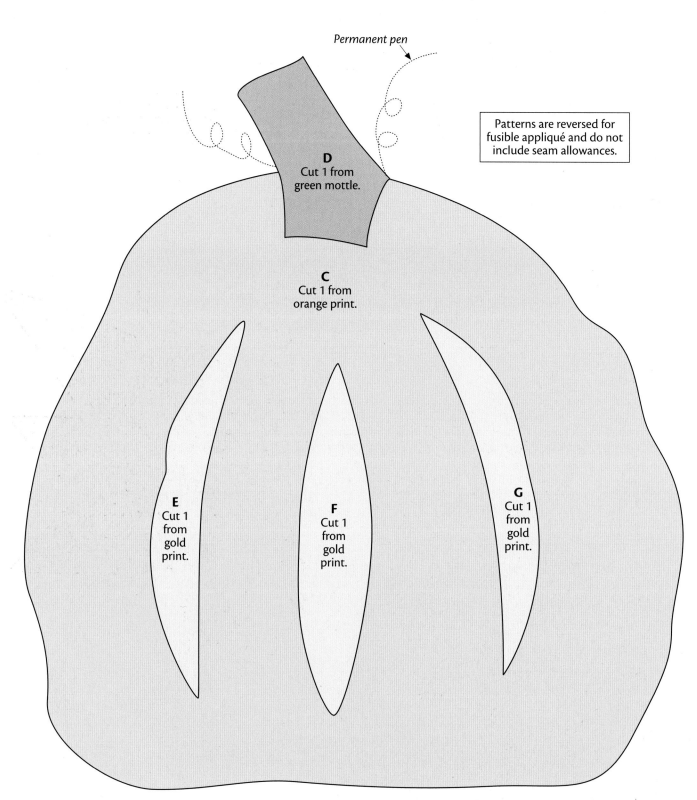

Permanent pen

Patterns are reversed for fusible appliqué and do not include seam allowances.

D
Cut 1 from green mottle.

C
Cut 1 from orange print.

E
Cut 1 from gold print.

F
Cut 1 from gold print.

G
Cut 1 from gold print.

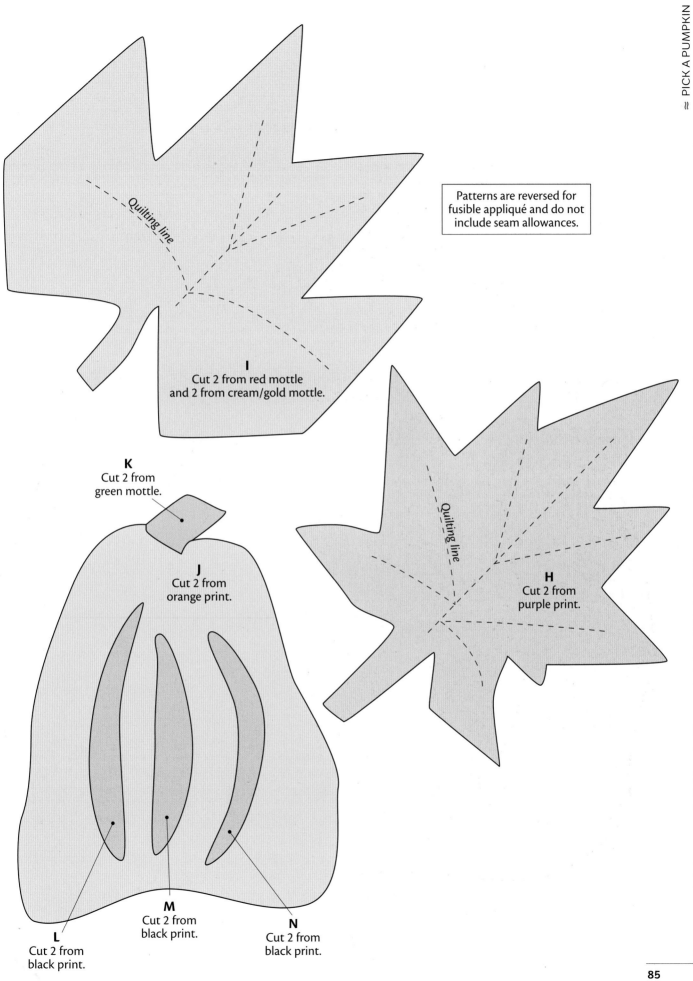

Patterns are reversed for fusible appliqué and do not include seam allowances.

Quilting line

I
Cut 2 from red mottle and 2 from cream/gold mottle.

Quilting line

H
Cut 2 from purple print.

K
Cut 2 from green mottle.

J
Cut 2 from orange print.

M
Cut 2 from black print.

L
Cut 2 from black print.

N
Cut 2 from black print.

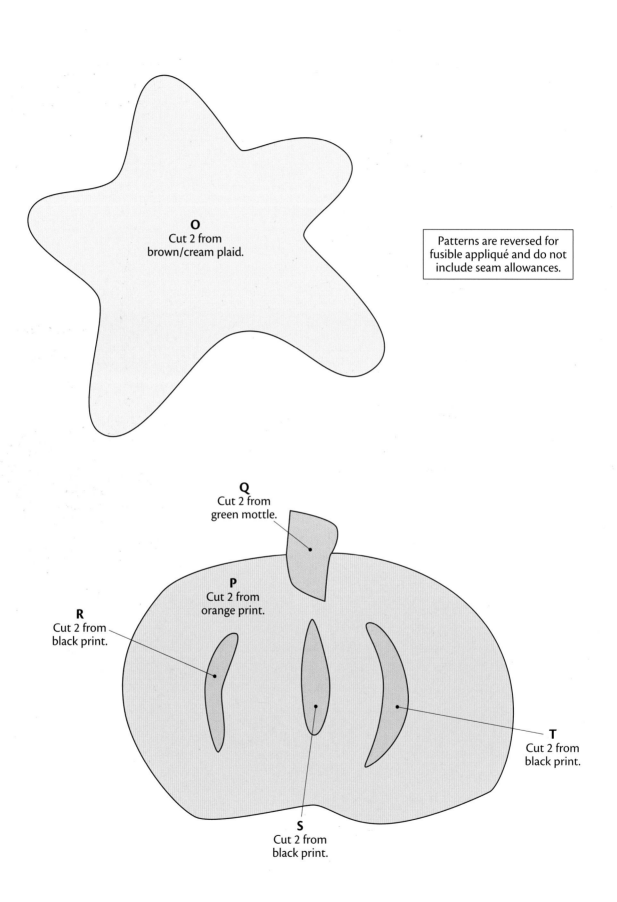

O
Cut 2 from
brown/cream plaid.

Patterns are reversed for
fusible appliqué and do not
include seam allowances.

Q
Cut 2 from
green mottle.

P
Cut 2 from
orange print.

R
Cut 2 from
black print.

T
Cut 2 from
black print.

S
Cut 2 from
black print.

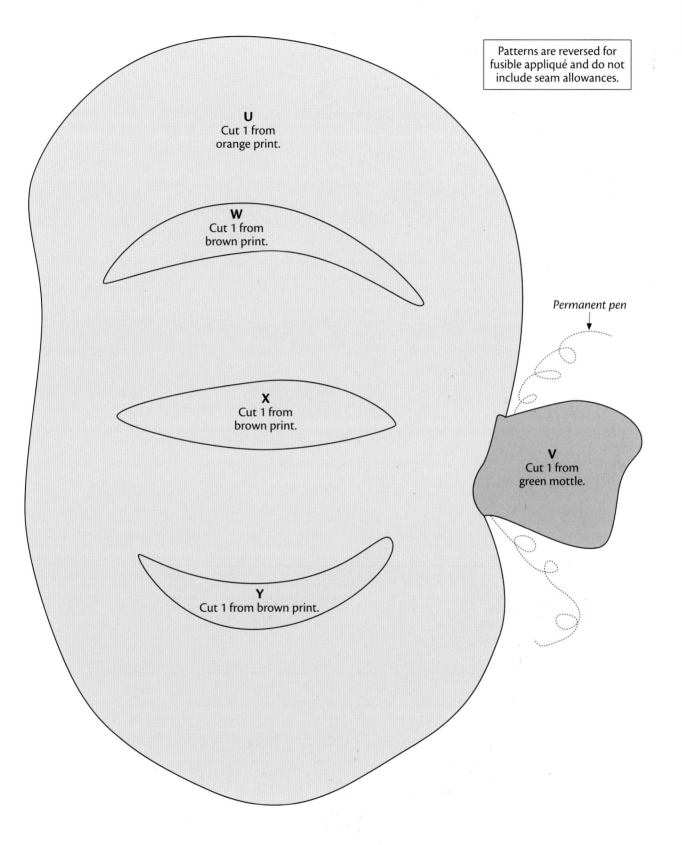

U
Cut 1 from
orange print.

W
Cut 1 from
brown print.

Patterns are reversed for
fusible appliqué and do not
include seam allowances.

Permanent pen

X
Cut 1 from
brown print.

V
Cut 1 from
green mottle.

Y
Cut 1 from brown print.

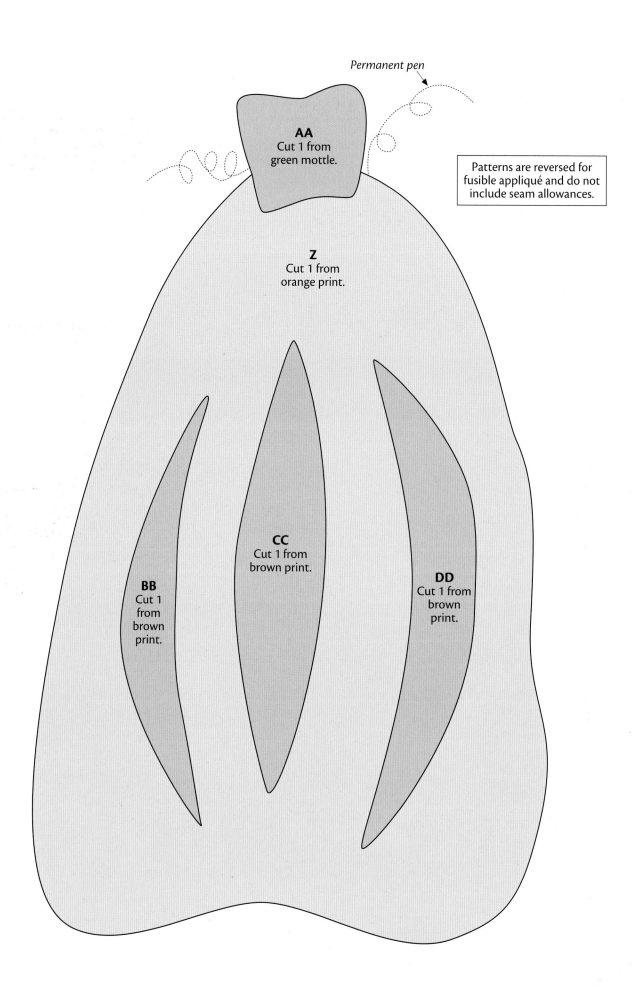

Permanent pen

AA
Cut 1 from
green mottle.

Patterns are reversed for
fusible appliqué and do not
include seam allowances.

Z
Cut 1 from
orange print.

CC
Cut 1 from
brown print.

BB
Cut 1
from
brown
print.

DD
Cut 1 from
brown
print.

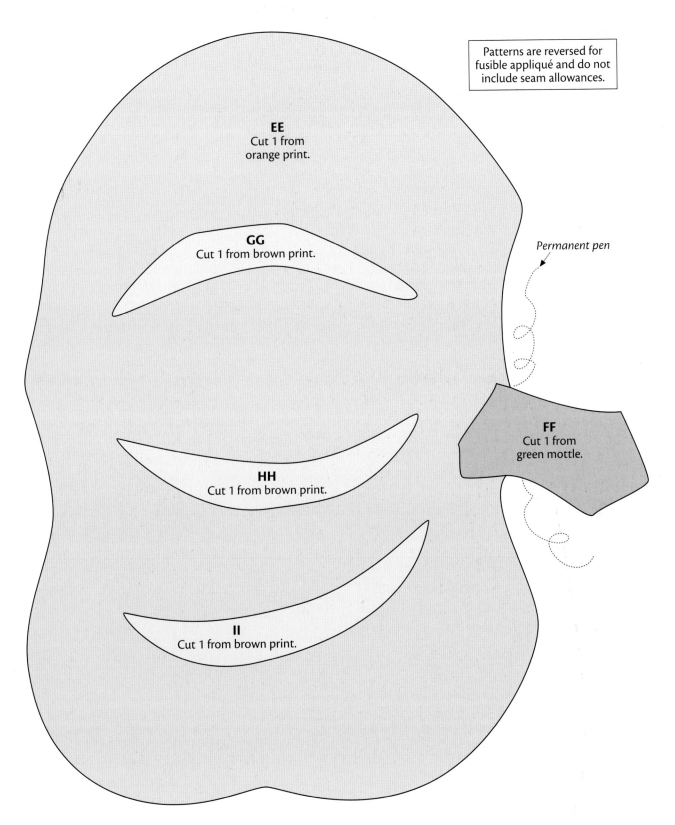

Patterns are reversed for fusible appliqué and do not include seam allowances.

EE
Cut 1 from
orange print.

GG
Cut 1 from brown print.

Permanent pen

HH
Cut 1 from brown print.

FF
Cut 1 from
green mottle.

II
Cut 1 from brown print.

QUILTMAKING BASICS

If you're new to quilting or just need a refresher, the following techniques will help you create the quilts in this book.

ROTARY CUTTING

For those unfamiliar with rotary cutting, a brief introduction is provided here.

1. To prepare the fabric, press to remove wrinkles. Fold the fabric and match selvages, aligning the crosswise and lengthwise grains as much as possible. Place the folded fabric on the cutting mat with the folded edge closest to you.

2. Align a square ruler along the folded edge of the fabric. Then place a long, straight ruler to the left of the square ruler, just covering the uneven raw edges of the left side of the fabric. Remove the square ruler and cut along the right edge of the long ruler, rolling the rotary cutter away from you. Discard this strip. (Reverse this procedure if you are left-handed.)

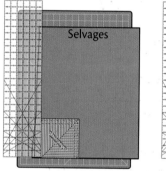

3. To cut strips, align the required measurement on the ruler with the newly cut edge of the fabric. For example, to cut a 3"-wide strip, place the 3" ruler mark on the edge of the fabric.

4. To cut squares or rectangles, cut strips in the required widths. Trim away the selvage ends. Align the required measurement on the ruler with the left edge of the strip and cut a square or rectangle.

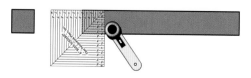

5. For half-square triangles, cut squares in half diagonally. For quarter-square triangles, cut squares into quarters diagonally.

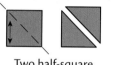

Two half-square triangles cut from one square

Four quarter-square triangles cut from one square

CUTTING BIAS STRIPS

1. Position the fabric on the grid side of the cutting mat so that the lengthwise and crosswise grains of the fabric align with the vertical and horizontal grid lines.

2. Begin cutting approximately 6" from the lower-left corner of the fabric. Align the 45° line on the ruler with the first horizontal grid line visible on the mat below the fabric's bottom edge. Make a cut, creating a waste triangle.

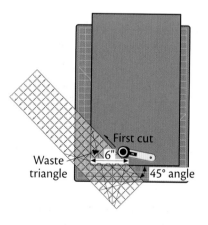

3. Align the required measurement on your ruler with the newly cut edge and cut the first strip.

4. Continue cutting until you have the number of strips required. Periodically recheck the position of the 45° angle marking on the ruler. If necessary, retrim the cut edge of the fabric to true up the angle.

MACHINE PIECING

The most important thing to remember about machine piecing is to maintain a consistent ¼"-wide seam allowance. This is necessary for the seams to match and for the resulting block or quilt to measure the desired finished size. Measurements for all components of each quilt are based on blocks that finish accurately to the desired size plus ¼" on each edge for seam allowances.

Take the time to establish an exact ¼"-wide seam guide on your machine. Some machines have a special quilting foot that measures exactly ¼" from the center needle position to the edge of the foot. If your machine doesn't have such a foot, create a seam guide by placing the edge of a piece of tape or moleskin ¼" away from the needle.

CHAIN PIECING

Chain piecing saves time and thread. It's helpful when you're sewing many identical units. Simply sew the first pair of pieces from cut edge to cut edge. At the end of the seam, stop sewing, but don't cut the thread. Feed the next pair of pieces under the presser foot, as close as possible to the first. Continue sewing without cutting the threads. When all the pieces are sewn, remove the chain from the machine, clip the threads, and press.

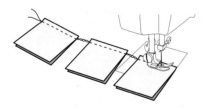

APPLIQUÉ

There are many techniques for appliqué and there's not space to cover all of them here. For additional information on other methods or more details, consult some of the many excellent books on the topic, or visit your local quilt shop to look into classes.

The first step for any method of appliqué except for fusible is to make a template either from plastic or from freezer paper. Plastic templates are more durable, and if one shape is repeated many times in the quilt, some quilters make a plastic template, which is then used to draw multiple freezer-paper templates. Freezer-paper templates will temporarily adhere to the fabric if the shiny side is placed face down on the fabric and pressed. You can reuse freezer-paper templates a few times before they will no longer stick to the fabric.

Basted-Edge Preparation

In this method, the edges of appliqué pieces are turned under and secured with a basting stitch before appliquéing by hand or machine.

1. Trace the appliqué pattern onto the dull side of freezer paper. Trace the pattern in reverse if it's asymmetrical and has not already been reversed for tracing. For symmetrical patterns, it doesn't matter.

2. Cut the freezer-paper template on the drawn lines and press it to the wrong side of the appliqué fabric.

3. Cut out the fabric shapes, adding a scant ¼" seam allowance around each shape.

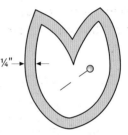

4. Turn the seam allowance over the edge of the paper and baste, close to the edge and through the paper. Clip the corners and baste the inner curves first. On outer curves, take small running stitches through the fabric only to ease in the fullness. Do not turn under edges that will be covered by another piece.

5. For sharp points, first fold the corner to the inside; then fold the remaining seam allowances over the paper.

Fold corners to inside.　　Fold remaining seam allowances over paper.

6 When all seam allowances are turned and basted, press the appliqués.

7 Pin and stitch the pieces to the background by machine (see "Machine Appliqué" on page 93) or by hand with the traditional appliqué stitch (see page 92).

8 After stitching, remove the basting stitches, *carefully* slit the background fabric behind the appliqué shape, and pull out the paper. Use tweezers if necessary to loosen the freezer paper.

Needle-Turn Hand Appliqué

With this technique, the edge of each piece is turned under with the edge of your needle as you stitch it to the background. Use a longer needle, such as a Sharp or milliner's, to help you control the seam allowance and turn it under as you stitch.

1 Place the template right side up on the right side of the fabric and trace around it with a No. 2 pencil or a white pencil, depending on your fabric color and print.

2 Cut the shape out, adding a scant ¼" seam allowance all around.

3 Pin or baste the appliqué piece in position on the background fabric.

4 Beginning on a straight edge, bring your needle up through the background and the appliqué piece, just inside the drawn line. Use the tip of the needle to gently turn under the seam allowance, about ½" at a time. Hold the turned seam allowance firmly between the thumb and first finger of one hand as you stitch the appliqué to the background fabric with your other hand. Use the traditional hand-appliqué stitch described below.

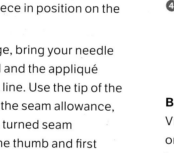

Traditional Hand-Appliqué Stitch

1 Thread a needle with a single strand of thread and knot one end. Use a thread color that matches the appliqué piece.

2 Slip the needle into the seam allowance from the wrong side of the appliqué, bringing it out on the fold line. Start the first stitch by inserting the needle into the background fabric right next to the folded edge of the appliqué where the thread exits the appliqué shape.

3 Let the needle travel under the background fabric, parallel to the edge of the appliqué; bring the needle up about ⅛" away through the edge of the appliqué, catching only one or two threads of the folded edge. Insert the needle into the background fabric right next to the folded edge. Let the needle travel under the background, and again, bring it up about ⅛" away, catching just the edge of the appliqué. Give the thread a slight tug and continue stitching.

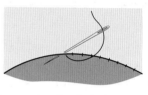

Appliqué stitch

4 Stitch around the appliqué, taking a couple of stitches beyond where you started. Knot the thread on the wrong side of the background fabric, behind the appliqué.

Bias Vines

Vines are narrow and curved, so it's best to cut them on the bias (see page 90). The width to cut the strips is given in the project instructions.

1 Fold the bias strips in half lengthwise, wrong sides together. Stitch ¼" from the raw edge and trim the seam allowance to ⅛".

2 Press the tube flat, centering the seam allowance on the back so the raw edge isn't visible from the front. Using a bias bar makes pressing faster and easier.

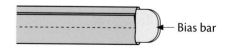

Bias bar

Machine Appliqué

For the least visible stitches, use monofilament thread—clear for light-colored appliqués or smoke for medium or dark colors—and a narrow zigzag stitch. If you want your stitches to show as a more decorative element, use a matching or contrasting-color thread in the top of your machine. Use a neutral-color thread to match your background fabric in the bobbin.

1 Set your machine for a small zigzag stitch (about ⅛" wide) and do a practice sample to test your stitches and tension. An open-toe presser foot is helpful for machine appliqué.

2 Prepare each appliqué piece using the basted-edge preparation method on page 91. Pin the pieces to the background and begin stitching with the pieces that are not overlapped by any other pieces.

3 Begin stitching with the needle just outside the appliqué piece and take two or three straight stitches in place to lock the thread. Make sure the needle is on the right of the appliqué and that the zigzag stitches will go into the appliqué piece. (You can use any decorative stitch on your machine.)

4 Stitch curved shapes slowly to maintain control, stopping and pivoting as needed.

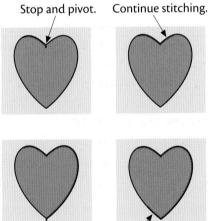

Stop and pivot.　　Continue stitching.

Stop and pivot.　　Continue stitching.

5 Stitch completely around the appliqué until you are slightly beyond the starting point. Take two or three straight stitches in place to lock the thread; clip the thread tails.

6 To remove the freezer paper, carefully trim away the background fabric behind the appliqué, leaving a generous ¼" seam allowance to keep your appliqué secure. Use tweezers as needed. (Bias stems and vines and fused appliqué shapes will not have paper to remove, so it's not necessary to cut away the background.)

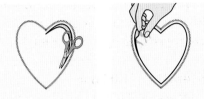

Fusible Appliqué

This appliqué method is fast and easy. Many fusing products are available for applying one piece of fabric to another, but fabrics do stiffen after application, so choose a lightweight fusible web. Follow the manufacturer's directions for the product you select. Unless the patterns are symmetrical or the pattern has already been reversed, you must reverse the templates when you draw them on the paper side of the fusible web. Do not add seam allowances to the appliqué pieces, but leave a ¼" to ½" cutting margin around each shape drawn on the fusible appliqué. For large appliqués, you can cut out the center of the fusible web, leaving a "donut" of web so that the centers of your appliqués will remain soft and unfused.

For quilts that will be washed often, finish the edges of the appliqués by stitching around them with a decorative stitch, such as a blanket stitch (by hand or machine) or zigzag stitch.

BORDERS

For best results, measure the quilt top before cutting and sewing the border strips to the quilt. Measure the quilt top through the center in both directions to determine how long to cut the border strips. This step ensures that the finished quilt will be as straight and as square as possible, without wavy edges.

Plain Borders

Many of these quilts call for plain border strips. Some of these strips are cut along the crosswise grain and joined where extra length is needed. Others are cut lengthwise and do not need to be pieced.

1 Measure the length of the quilt top through the center. Cut two borders to this measurement. Determine the midpoints of the border and quilt top by folding them in half and creasing or pinning the centers. Then pin the borders to opposite sides of the quilt top, matching the center marks and ends and easing as necessary. Sew the border strips in place. Press the seam allowances toward the borders.

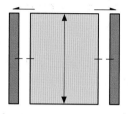

Measure center of quilt,
top to bottom. Mark centers.

2 Measure the width of the quilt top through the center, including the side borders just added. Cut two borders to this measurement. Mark the centers of the quilt edges and the border strips. Pin the borders to the top and bottom edges of the quilt top, matching the center marks and ends and easing as necessary. Sew the border strips in place. Press the seam allowances toward the borders.

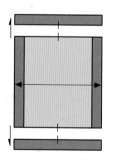

Measure center of quilt, side to side,
including border strips. Mark centers.

Mitered Borders

1 Starting and stopping ¼" from the quilt corners and backstitching to secure, sew the border strips to the quilt top. Press the seam allowances toward the quilt center.

2 Fold the quilt on the diagonal at one corner, right sides together. Align the border-strip raw edges and border seams at the ¼" backstitched point; pin together.

3 Align a ruler edge with the fold, extending the ruler completely across the border. Draw a line from the backstitched point to the border raw edges. Stitch along the drawn line, backstitching at both ends. Press the seam allowances open.

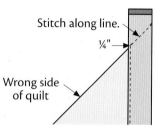

Stitch along line.

¼"

Wrong side
of quilt

4 With the quilt right side up, align the 45°-angle line of the ruler on the seam line to check accuracy. If the corner is flat and square, trim the excess fabric to a ¼" seam allowance. Repeat for all corners.

45°

Right side
of quilt

FINISHING

The quilt "sandwich" consists of backing, batting, and the quilt top. Cut the quilt backing 4" to 6" longer and wider than the quilt top. Baste the layers together with thread for hand quilting or safety pins for machine quilting. Quilt by hand or machine.

Hand Quilting

To quilt by hand, you'll need short, sturdy needles (called Betweens), quilting thread, and a thimble to fit the middle finger of your sewing hand. Most quilters also use a frame or hoop to support their work.

1 Thread a needle with a single strand of quilting thread, knot one end, and insert the needle in the top layer about 1" from the place where you want to start stitching. Pull the needle out at the point where quilting will begin and gently pull the thread until the knot pops through the fabric and into the batting.

2 Take small, evenly spaced stitches through all three quilt layers. Rock the needle up and down through all layers until you have three or four stitches on the needle. Place your other hand under the quilt so that you can feel the needle point with the tip of your finger when a stitch is taken. Pull the thread through so it lies evenly on the fabric, being careful not to pull too tight.

3 To end a line of quilting, make a small knot close to the last stitch; then backstitch, running the thread a needle's length through the batting. Gently pull the thread until the knot pops into the batting; clip the thread at the quilt's surface.

Machine Quilting

For straight-line quilting, it's extremely helpful to have a walking foot to help feed the quilt layers through the machine without shifting or puckering. Some machines have a built-in walking foot; other machines require a separate attachment. Read the machine's instruction manual for special tension settings to sew through extra fabric thicknesses.

For curved designs or stippling, use a darning foot and lower the feed dogs for free-motion quilting. Free-motion quilting allows the fabric to move freely under the foot of the sewing machine. Because the feed dogs are lowered, the stitch length is determined by the speed at which you run the machine and feed the fabric under the foot. Practice on scraps until you get the feel of controlling the motion of the fabric with your hands.

Cutting Continuous Bias Strips from a Square

This technique provides a long strip of bias binding without having to sew individual pieces together. Bias binding strips are stretchier than straight-grain binding and are used for curved and wavy quilt edges. Bias binding also rotates stripes and plaids so they run on the diagonal as in "Rambling Rose" on page 18.

1 Remove the selvages from the fabric and cut a square as directed in the project instructions. (A 40" square should make about 16 yards of 2½"-wide bias strip.)

2 Lightly label the square as shown. Cut the square in half diagonally to make triangles.

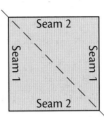

3 With right sides together and raw edges aligned, join the triangles (seam 1) to form a parallelogram. Press the seam allowances open. Measure and mark across the parallelogram with lines equal to the width of your bias strip as shown.

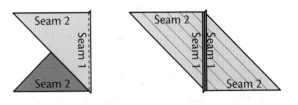

4 Form a tube by aligning the edges marked seam 2, matching your marked lines and offsetting the edge one strip width beyond the line. Stitch and press the seam allowances open.

5 Starting at the offset end, cut around the tube on the marked lines to make a continuous bias strip.

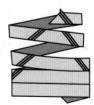

Binding

The quilt directions tell you how wide to cut the strips for binding. Bindings are generally cut anywhere from 2" to 2½" wide, depending on personal preference. You'll need enough strips to go around the perimeter of the quilt plus 12". If you cut a continuous bias binding strip, begin the following instructions in step 2.

1. Sew the strips together end to end to make one long piece of binding. Join the strips at right angles and stitch from corner to corner. Trim the excess fabric and press the seam allowances open.

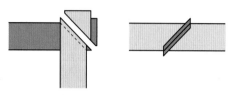

2. Trim one end of the binding strip at a 45° angle. Turn under ¼" and press.

3. Fold the strip in half lengthwise, wrong sides together, and press.

Fold line

4. Trim the batting and backing even with the edges of the quilt top.

5. Starting in the middle of one side and using a ¼"-wide seam allowance, stitch the binding to the quilt. Keep the raw edges even with the quilt-top edge. Begin stitching 1" to 2" from the start of the binding. End the stitching ¼" from the corner of the quilt and backstitch. Clip the thread.

6. Turn the quilt so that you'll be stitching along the next side. Fold the binding up, away from the quilt; then fold it back down onto itself, even with the raw edge of the quilt top.

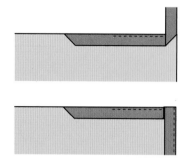

7. Stitch from the fold of the binding along the second edge of the quilt top, stopping ¼" from the corner as before. Repeat the stitching and mitering process on the remaining edges and corners.

8. When you reach the starting point, cut the end 1" longer than needed and tuck the end inside the beginning. Stitch the rest of the binding.

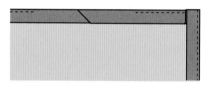

9. Fold the binding over the raw edges of the quilt to the back and blindstitch in place.